QUEER PEOPLE

QUEER PEOPLE

by

DOUGLAS PLUMMER

Introduction by Donald Webster Cory

The Citadel Press
NEW YORK

The author gratefully acknowledges the assistance of the Homosexual Law Reform Society in the preparation of material for the writing of this book.

FIRST AMERICAN EDITION, 1965

Published by The Citadel Press, 222 Park Avenue South, New York, N. Y. 10003. Manufactured in the United States of America. Library of Congress Catalog Card No.: 65-15494

Introduction

"A FOREIGNER can photograph the exterior of a nation, but I think that that is as far as he can get. I think that no foreigner can report its interior—its soul, its life, its speech, its thought. I think that a knowledge of these things is acquirable in only one way—not two or four or six—*absorption;* years and years of unconscious absorption, of living it, indeed; sharing personally in its shames and prides, its joys and griefs, its loves and hates . . ."

Thus wrote Mark Twain, and unhappy though he might have been to know the use to which these words are now being put, I can think of no statement that makes a more fitting introduction to this little book. It is, in fact, more than an introduction; it is its justification.

Since World War II, a powerful spotlight has been focussed throughout the Western world on the problem of the homosexual. Among many factors that created a new social climate for investigation of this subject were the increased interest in and sympathy for all those suffering from emotional difficulties that came in the wake of the Freudian revolution; the revolt against Victorian morality and the breakdown of many of its hypocritical pretences that grew into the sexual revolution; the new awareness on the part of a large public that homosexuals are so numerous that they can appear in one's own family or in the house next door (an awareness intensified by the publicity given to the Kinsey report); and the widespread association of homosexuals with minority groups, in an era when people saw the minority as being the wronged and not the wrongdoers.

It was in this climate that jurists, clergymen, psychologists—and, in fact, homosexuals as well—began to re-examine the validity and social usefulness of legislation that makes many millions of otherwise law-abiding citizens into lawbreakers. It was in the course of this re-examination that a powerful document came forth in England: the Wolfenden Report. And, for the first time in history, organizations were being formed, in England and in the United States, urging social reform in the public attitude toward the sexually deviant. In England, the best-known of these groups is the Homosexual Law Reform Society; in America they include several organizations called Mattachine Society or having similar names, a Janus Society, a woman's group called Daughters of Bilitis, and the publication *One,* along with several others that may or may not prove short-lived.

And out of this has come a great deal of literature, some helpful, some insightful, but much that is only the photograph of the exterior by the foreigner. Only occasionally has someone been able to report the interior: the soul, the life, the years of living it, "its shames and prides, its joys and griefs, its loves and hates."

It is this task to which Douglas Plummer addresses himself, forthrightly, interestingly, and competently. Competently, because he states his credentials: he is one of them, he is one of the "queer people" of whom he writes, and he imparts to his writing the feeling of one who is living it. He is far from the first to so do: to name only a few, there was Proust, utilizing the medium of the novel; Gide, in his philosophical dialogues; Hirschfeld, who refused to commit himself publicly to his subjective involvement; and Edward Carpenter, product of mid-Victorian romanticism. To these I might add my own efforts and those of colleagues and a collaborator.

But what makes Douglas Plummer's work unique is that it is a subjective approach to the feelings and life of the homosexual as he is found in the England of Wolfenden and of the Homosexual Law Reform Society. This is what it means to be one of them—nay, one of *us*—in the land where this topic is rocking the halls of Parliament, where its legal ramifications are debated daily, where several arrests and convictions received nation-wide and even world-wide attention, and where an organization supported by many of the country's leading intellectuals is openly espousing a cause that was but recently unmentionable.

For all the pronunciamentos of lawmakers, all the deepgoing sympathy of clergymen (who often compound the difficulty by emphasizing the sinfulness of homosexual activity while calling for the lifting of legal sanctions on it), and all the perceptive analyses of psychiatrists who have studied a few cases in detail—all these can mean little unless related to the Douglas Plummers, to the people who are repeating to themselves, in an endless inner monologue, the words with which he opens his book: *I am a homosexual, a so-called "queer" or "pansy."*

For a problem is real when it ceases to be a statistic and is translated into human beings. And this is what comes through in Plummer's work: one person, one human being, searching for the meaning of his life and for a means of accommodating to a hostile society. If we can take his study and multiply it by several millions, without losing the individual in the mass, but seeing the mass as made up of individuals, then we can begin to sympathize with these people.

I, too, like Plummer, write under a pseudonym, for I, too, am homosexual. But his work expresses for me the specific meaning of the outlook of the homosexual in the Queen's England of the nineteen-sixties. It is a life bedevilled by fear, haunted by the police and the blackmailer, driving people to suicide, and then creating the reaction against this deplorable social condition: the movement to change the law. With simplicity and understanding, the author of this book reflects the England in which he lives and in which he hides. If he did not, the book would have little value.

From my own vantage point, however, I cannot believe that the legal aspect is an especially significant factor in the difficulties of the homosexual in society. If, as I confidently expect, the Homosexual Law Reform Society and its many friends and colleagues should be successful in implementing the Wolfenden Report and, in some modified manner, having its major provisions enacted into law, the difficulties of the homosexual will not automatically be solved. In fact, there are many parts of the world, as the author points out, where there are no legal penalties for homosexual activity; and in one state of the United States even public solicitation for the purpose of engaging in such activity (in private) is not illegal. Nevertheless, in that state and in numerous other parts of the world the lot of the homosexual is not substantially different from his unfortunate position in England. Why? Because his difficulties are not primarily legal in origin. They are personal (or psychological, if you will) and they are social. The personal and the social certainly are interrelated, feeding one another, compounding the problem, and in this situation, a legal problem is not easy to handle.

No one wants to be blackmailed or to go to jail for activities which he considers proper and right. But the problem of the homosexual is that he must himself consider these activities moral and right if he is to have an image of himself as a worthwhile person and if he is to convey this image to a hostile society. In order to achieve such a view of himself, and equally important, of his friends, associates, and lovers, he must be able to look at society generally, and at the significant people in his family and other close groups, and see himself being accepted for what he is—rather than for what he is not.

The great value of this book, and of the Society whose remarkable activities it describes, is that, in marshalling the opinion of the public in favor of *legal* change, they are aiding in the remolding of public opinion in order to bring about *social* change. Few documents that have come out of Britain in recent years, in this era of Wolfenden and Wildeblood, of Kinsey and Mattachine, can be as important as a work that stops to tell us: *I am a homosexual and I am a human being.*

DONALD WEBSTER CORY

Foreword

THIS is a personal survey of homosexuality in Britain today. One of the worst effects of the continued persecution of homosexuals under the existing English laws has been to make many of us doubt and mistrust ourselves. We are made to feel guilty, although we did not choose our condition. And we tend to accept, quietly and willingly, the ignorant ridicule and discrimination which is levelled against us.

Sometimes we even imagine that our lot is not without justification. This little book is an attempt to spread the truth, to enlighten the uninformed, and to help those many people who are homosexual.

I have used the word "queer" often in the text, as well as in the title. My reason is that I want the book to be read by people who will understand what "queer" means, but might fight shy of the word homosexual. "Queer" is an unfortunately defensive word, indicating that we are somehow beyond the pale of ordinary society. That we are in fact an important part of society, I shall presently explain.

The original meaning of the word "queer" was base, criminal, counterfeit, or inferior. The first known printed use of the word was in Scotch, in 1508, when it meant odd, eccentric, or of questionable character. Thus, to be "in queer" was to be in wrong with the police, and in the seventeenth century to be a "queer bird" was to have been only recently let out of jail but already returned to crime. Today, many people in Britain know the word as meaning homosexual, and nothing else.

I originally wrote this book as a series of short articles intended for a popular newspaper. I believed that what I wished to say was important and should be widely read. So I sent the articles first to a Sunday newspaper. After about a fortnight the editor returned them saying he agreed with everything I had written, he thought the articles should be published, he had found them "well written and very moving", but unfortunately the time was not yet ripe for their publication in a newspaper. Public opinion was not ready for them.

I then delivered the articles to another Sunday newspaper. I had always imagined that writers and publishers and editors guided or led public opinion in matters of social importance. But I was wrong. This time the articles came back with a letter saying they were well worth publishing, but that the policy of that particular influential group was against them. The editor added a personal note saying he thought I would have no difficulty in getting them published elsewhere. Such was my faith in human nature that I believed him.

I tried two other newspapers before finally sending the articles to a weekly journal which has in the past righted many wrongs and frequently championed the oppressed. This time my rejection letter came from a member of the staff who said he realised that "this disease" was spreading, but that it "frankly sickened him", so that he could not publish what I had written. Clearly, he hadn't read my text, and I couldn't be bothered to tell him that our condition is not a "disease", is not "spreading", and that his ignorance frankly sickened *me*.

Since then I have made more enquiries, and I have found evidence of this ignorance in all walks of life. It is clear that the majority of people, even well-educated people, know very little about homosexuals or their problems, which in this country are acute.

I decided to expand and rewrite the articles in volume form, not as a medical or text book, but in simple, everyday language to appeal to a majority of readers, setting down frankly what I know about my condition, the homosexuals I have met, and what I have been able to discover, through research and study, about the world of the homosexual. There is, of course, a great deal more which could be said, but this is a beginning.

Contents

Change the law, purify that murky atmosphere, bring Britain into line with civilisation and this bogey, with many others, will vanish

J. B. PRIESTLEY

CHAPTER 1

I am not Ashamed

I

I AM a homosexual, a so-called "queer" or "pansy". I admit it without shame, although I must hide behind a false name because of fear of the law, vindictiveness, and ignorance. I am a respectable citizen with a good job and a decent record. I volunteered for the Army directly war was declared in 1939 and I was an Infantry Officer for six years, fighting in three major tank battles, in the last of which I was wounded.

If you met me you would not know I was homosexual. Nine out of ten of us are indistinguishable from our fellows, in appearance, dress, or general behaviour. We are certainly not all effeminate "pansies" in appearance. Furthermore, you may be surprised to know that there are at least a million men like me in Britain, some say nearly two million. And of course there are many millions more in other countries. At least four per cent of the population of the United Kingdom is "queer", and there is every indication that this figure remains fairly constant. That is, at least a million men and a million women.

We male homosexuals feel it is perfectly natural to love a man instead of a woman. But unfortunately for us the law of England, as it stands at present, is against our love, and too few people understand us. For this reason I have studied my own condition and wish to reveal what I know and have discovered about what Lord Alfred Douglas called "the love that dare not speak its name".

I believe this love should now be accepted and should be freely discussed in schools and family circles and everywhere where social problems are debated. There is nothing unusual about it. It is part of the natural pattern of life. But not all homosexuals fully understand their condition, especially when they are young and have no-one to advise them. Therefore I shall tell the truth, frankly.

Homosexuality or "queerness" is not a kind of behaviour, or a disease, or a vice. It is a condition, like having a hare lip, or small ankles, or thick lips, or bad eyesight, or large ears. It is not a habit, like smoking, which may be acquired and broken again if the will is strong. It is not a practice which can be spread, or caught, or picked up in schools, and it is not necessarily the result of an all-male environment. Neither is it "wicked" nor "sinful" nor "bad" nor "dirty" to be homosexual, any more than it is wrong to have one arm longer than the other or to be left-handed.

Our condition is not, as has been suggested, due to glandular trouble. All men and women and animals have a certain supply of both male and female hormones in their bodies, but there is no scientific reason for believing that a homosexual has an over-abundant supply of the hormones of the opposite sex, or an inadequate supply of those of his own sex.[1]

We do not choose our condition, which is simply that we are attracted by our own sex instead of the opposite sex. But this is nothing unusual, for all men and women, at some time in their lives, have tendencies in this direction. Scientifically and medically there is nothing unnatural about it, and certainly nothing strange. Evidence of "queer" behaviour exists throughout the world among humans and animals, and always has. But only in a few remaining free countries are *private* sexual acts between consenting adults regarded as criminal. These countries are the United States, Western Germany, Britain, and most of the Com-

[1] *Sex and the Adolescent*, by Maxine Davis.

monwealth countries. Nearly everywhere else, we are recognised and helped.

You need not shudder or feel sorry for me. I don't feel sorry for myself. I should be perfectly happy if public opinion understood and accepted my condition, which is not of my choosing, but which is shared by so many people.

My love for my kind is just as deep as the love of the average man for the woman of his choice. Certainly it is just as intense. Nowadays this love is more openly discussed than in Oscar Wilde's time, but it is still not fully understood in Britain.

It is extraordinary how ignorant and intolerant some people are about our problem. A South London newspaper, in a crowded area where there are, by the law of averages, many homosexuals, recently printed the headline: GET TOUGH WITH THE PANSIES! It suggested that when we "queers" use the word "love" it becomes a "dirty" word.

A great misfortune of our times still persisting, although perhaps less harshly than in Victorian days, is the holding of *all* sexuality to be a "dirty business", not to be discussed openly, hardly to be whispered. Emotionally, it is considered "wrong", disreputable, unclean. Even normal co-habitation, the mating act between married couples, is regarded by many people as unmentionable. How much more difficult it is, therefore, for some people to face and understand the facts about homosexuality.

I recently heard of two Liverpool men who lived together for fifty years. When the older man was seventy he died. So his friend drowned himself, feeling unable to face the future alone. And in Australia the distinguished thirty-one-year-old pianist Noel Mewton-Wood committed suicide following the death of "a very dear friend" who had died of appendicitis. Can you honestly say that such affection is not worthy and sincere?

Many homosexual friendships, like heterosexual or so-called "normal" ones, do not include physical acts. And as I shall explain later, all homosexuals are certainly not perverts. The average "queer", when he first becomes aware of the tendencies in his nature, is usually young and ignorant, and often has no-one to guide him but the other boys in the street, or at school, or in the factory. He is shocked and bewildered and unhappy, imagining for some time that he is the only person in the world with such strange feelings. Is he sick? Has he caught some disease? What is wrong? He needs sound advice and help but he seldom gets it. Very often his doctor, or the local parson, or his friends, know very little about homosexuality—even if he can bear to reveal his fears.

Perhaps with time, if he is fortunate and especially if he meets others like him, he may be able to adjust himself to his condition and learn to live at peace with himself and the seemingly hostile world around him. And in Britain, for at least a million of us, it is often a very hostile world. Imagine what it must seem like to a sensitive boy in his 'teens whose parents will not understand, who is too illiterate or afraid to go to his local library to find out more about his condition, who has been taught nothing about it except what he has picked up in the streets, who fears that he is not fully what all his mates boast of being—a real man.

II

Until 1885 English law was concerned only with sodomy and indecency in public, but in that year a Bill was introduced to "make further provision for the protection of women and girls" and for "the suppression of brothels". Henry Labouchère, M.P., moved the introduction of a new clause making indecent acts between males in public *or in private* a criminal offence. Another M.P. asked if it was in order to introduce this new clause into the Bill, but the Speaker ruled that it was up to the House to decide, and the new clause was accordingly accepted without debate or discussion or further thought. From that day on, all sexual acts between males, even in the privacy of bedrooms between consenting adults, became criminal offences punishable by two years' imprisonment. The change in the law has since been called "the blackmailer's charter".

Strictly speaking it is not a legal offence in English law to be a homosexual. But it is a serious offence for males to practise sexual acts together, even in private. It is an offence (with a two-year prison penalty) for a man to take part in any so-called "act of gross indecency" with another man, even in the dark behind locked doors, and even many years after the event. That is to say, both men can be sent to jail several years after it happened, once it is discovered and proved. It is also an offence in the case of two eight-year-olds, but the law has always been tolerant about this.

Until recently most Britons were content to imagine, or pretend, that homosexuality was unusual. Perhaps it is part of our national character to stick our heads into the sand and ignore what is really happening in the outside world. But now more people are beginning to realise that the condition of homosexuality is right next door and often in the same house. With at least a million of us in Britain, *you* probably know at least one homosexual. It could be your own son or brother or uncle. Homosexuality is no respecter of persons. I know several fathers who are practising "queers", and they can't do anything to change their way of life. I don't merely mean that they can't overcome their condition, but also that there is no known *cure* for them. Can you lengthen the arm of a man who was born with one longer than the other?

I was a schoolboy when I discovered that I was homosexual. It happens to many boys, and most of them get over it. But I didn't. For some time I thought I was ill, or incurably mad. Now I know I am no more ill or mad than the 'bus conductor who collects my fares or the television announcer who reads the news. But I have learned that to be "queer" in Britain today means that one is often outside the law and beyond normal society, simply because of the ignorance of people who know very little about us, yet persecute us and call us "filthy degenerates".

Most "queers" think and behave exactly like anyone else in all matters except love. And unless we are of the rare, extremely effeminate type who wears very colourful clothes and bright colours, we cannot be distinguished from so-called "normal" people.

The truth is that there are really no "normal" people. Each man's desires vary a little from those of his neighbour. There are only degrees of what we loosely call "normality". No two people in the world are exactly alike, just as no two flowers and no two animals are alike. It would be a dull world if we were all the same. Indeed, this is one of the wonders of the world, that life is so varied, so unpredictable.

Sir John Wolfenden has pointed out that it is a serious mistake to think of the human race as being divided neatly into two clear categories—homosexuals on the left and so-called "normals" on the right. People and animals and birds and even insects and fish are much more mixed-up than that, and always have been. What is more, we must all learn to live together.

III

I sometimes think we homosexuals are absurdly tolerant. The way some newspapers attack us would not be accepted by any other group of a million people. Imagine the Quakers or the Christian Scientists or all the redheads or even all the hunchbacks being reviled and sent to jail.

Although it is not of our choosing, our condition is frequently described in certain newspapers as being "a filthy vice", "the West End vice", "an unpleasant freemasonry", "a secret brotherhood", "a chi-chi world", and a "social disease". I quote from actual press cuttings. Responsible, educated journalists who should know better have called us "pansies" and "lilies" and "perverts". If homosexuals stopped buying those particular newspapers, some circulations would drop by many hundreds of thousands of copies. Intolerance, ignorance, and lack of understanding is no excuse for abusing us.

Although there are so many of us in these islands, and throughout the Commonwealth (as in all other lands), we are, compared with the world population, a relatively small community. It is therefore easy for us to get to know one another. Experience sometimes tells us if another man is "queer". It has been suggested that we operate as a cult, and I have read of powerful homosexual secret societies, but this is all nonsense. There are no such societies and there is no secret organisation. In fact, we are completely disorganised and rather pathetically fail to speak with one voice, being absurdly afraid of public censure. Yet a million or more voices should not be negligible, if raised in defence of a way of life which the world is powerless to alter.

In Britain the only thing that draws us together is the feeling of being unwanted outcasts. The law, the police, many magistrates, and far too many newspapers—all combine to make us feel unwanted. We therefore tend to meet in private houses, at parties, in drinking clubs, coffee bars, and public houses, to be with our kind. For many of us, a satisfactory home life is denied. The feeling of being outside the law, a suppressed minority, *drives* us together in places where we hope the police and uninformed public opinion will leave us alone.

Most "queers" genuinely want, and mentally and physically need, to settle down happily with another homosexual in what we call and regard as a "married" state. Those of us fortunate enough to achieve this—and many do—in spite of the fierce opposition of the outside world and the taboos and superstitions and conventions of society, refer to one another as being "married" or as being "affairs". Like all humans and animals we need affection, understanding, and companionship from our own kind in order to live full, responsible lives. Yet the English law *denies* a full life to at least a million of her subjects. Society commands us to hide our true feelings. Many of us are condemned to lead unhappy, frustrated lives. Can you wonder that many "queers" are neurotic? Could you hide *your* feelings and hopes and desires day after day and year after year from the people with whom you work, or from your family?

Imagine the everyday pretence we are forced to endure, the lies, half-truths, explanations to parents and employers and friends who are unlikely to understand or accept the truth. Consider the thoughts which must be bottled up, the guilt complexes thrust upon us—and all because so many people are ignorant or apathetic about us, or can't be bothered to understand us, or have never been told.

Compared with many like me, I have been lucky. For nearly a quarter of a century I lived with one person. We enjoyed a full "married" life such as is often denied many men and women. My "queer" friends regard me as fortunate, for it is what we all seek. Yet everything was against our union. During our long partnership—which ended only with his death—we could not express our love in public. We couldn't even hold hands like other couples in love. We had to keep up a constant pretence. And although we lived decent, moral lives, and were respected members of our local community, our relationship could not be blessed by the Church, and was condemned by the laws of the State. We could have no wedding ring, no bonds except our faith and our determination. But we prayed together, kneeling side by side unashamed by the bedside, and because our faith was strong—I believe—we learned to overcome many of the obstacles. We tried never to offend against society, but to live like any married couples would, sharing the same home and the same interests. In most ways, we succeeded.

I have many friends who struggle to stay together and be happy, just as we did. It is far more difficult than for married men and women, and the dice are loaded heavily against us, but many achieve what we seek, to lead full, contented lives together. Sometimes parents and brothers and sisters understand the position, possibly without ever mentioning it (so strange are humans about this most human of conditions!), and then the path seems easier. Many parents close their eyes, realising that this is the only solution, for George or Tom or Harry to love and live with someone who returns his love. Yet I, and possibly George or Tom or Harry, could all have been sent to prison many times for having dared to live with the person of our choice.

It is nearly always enriching to be loved, and to return love. Yet our union was strictly illegal, and many men go to jail every year for a great deal less than living with another man for twenty-two years. Some go to jail for only two minutes' sudden display of affection, often after a lifetime of enforced celibacy. Over eighty per cent of convictions for homosexual first offences concern men who can bear enforced celibacy no longer, and unexpectedly, tragically, "break out".

Are you surprised that some "queers" lead promiscuous lives? It is often so much less obvious, and safer, than a permanent relationship. Yet the majority of us are not more promiscuous than so-called "normal" folk, although we have many more difficulties to contend with. Just as there are prostitutes, so of course there are male prostitutes, but they are only a tiny fraction of the homosexual population.

It seems to me illogical that "queer" affairs are not accepted, because except where married men or women are involved, which is very seldom, homosexual behaviour between adults is far less socially disruptive than adultery, and homosexuals hardly ever break up families.

I know two young men who were determined to start their partnership with a stronger bond than mere affection. They were proud of one another, and they wanted their love to last, as all lovers do. So they arranged a wedding ceremony in a private house, invited their friends, and standing before a table adorned as a simple altar, they swore fidelity to each other. Then their friends gathered round and drank to their happiness. Their feelings were genuine. It was a gay occasion. They knew the world was against them, so they sought to grasp something of the mysterious, elusive security of marriage. Some might think it blasphemous, but can you honestly say that it was disgusting, or degrading, bearing in mind that both men were incapable of so-called "normal" relationships?

In the Wolfenden Report, which recommended a revision of the law which sends us to prison, we were classed with prostitutes, as if being "queer" was a vice. Yet nowhere does the Bible suggest that our so-called moral "sin" should be punished by civil law.

Every day in Britain, many "queers" go to jail, although we are quite unable to stop being what we are, and all the doctors in the world still have no cure for us. In fact, most doctors know very little about our problems, and many give absurd advice.

One reason why many people think homosexuality is a crime is that they imagine it weakens our loyalty to our country, and that it has caused the downfall of great nations. But this is an old wives' tale. The English law against us was not introduced until 1885, when Britain was at the peak of her power as a world influence. The greatness of Britain was built up when homosexuality *wasn't* illegal. And the story that homosexuality caused the downfall of the Greek and Roman Empires is a myth. In fact, as I shall show you, some of our greatest Empire builders, and a great many of our humanitarians, have been homosexual.

It has been suggested that we are inclined to be loyal to ourselves, disloyal to the community, and "bad security risks". But in fact the majority of us are not concerned with politics, and yet are intensely loyal. The war records of individual "queers", both in the fighting services and in civil defence and administration, prove that—especially in social work—we are valuable and important members of the community.

What, then, do we expect?

We want to be recognised and tolerated, not abused and thrown into jail for being something we cannot help and science cannot cure. We wish to be integrated into society, and to be allowed those measures of freedom which should not be denied civilised people. Only then can progress be made in discovering more about our condition, and only then can we play our full, and not unimportant, part in human society. As I shall show you, it happens in many other countries. So why not here?

CHAPTER 2

Who are We?

I

WE homosexuals have no secret signs, but when we meet and talk together, we have our own slang expressions, which are generally unknown to the outside world, and of course vary in different languages, and constantly change. In Edwardian times a homosexual was said to be "so" or "like that". In America he is known as "gay". In Britain today a homosexual who looks masculine is described as being "butch", while an effeminate type is called "bitch". To prostitute oneself for money—which is rare in the homosexual world—is to be "rent". "Married" homosexual couples are usually called "affairs", and there is an unwritten code of honour which respects such partnerships as if we were really married. The word "drag" refers to women's clothes if worn by men. To "send up" is to ridicule. A Lesbian is called a "tom" or a "dyke" or "dike". The sexual act is described by more promiscuous or uneducated homosexuals as "having trade". The Elizabethan word "quean" is frequently used, but has degenerated into "queen". And when a homosexual uses the word "camp" he means "theatrically effeminate". Not only people but also clothes and behaviour and decoration can be described as "camp", and the expression is now used increasingly and indiscriminately by theatre folk.

However, by no means all homosexuals know these terms, or use them. Most of us are very ordinary people, and the majority of us suppress or control our feelings, especially outside the big cities. A recent police "witch-hunt" in Kirkcaldy, Scotland, revealed the occupations of six homosexuals who had come to know one another. They were a miner, a labourer, a garage works manager, a bookmaker, a furniture salesman, and a 'bus conductor. Another case at Taunton involved nineteen men of all classes and professions and occupations. Questions and cross-examinations and threats and sometimes promises of leniency had led the police from one man to another, involving relationships going back many months. The judge said he was appalled at the "extraordinary amount" of homosexual behaviour in Somerset. Almost any "queer" could have told him that it is no worse in Somerset than anywhere else. In fact, because of the relatively sparse population there are probably fewer homosexuals there. But the Somerset police were active against them, and they probed deep. It is not difficult to find homosexuals if houses are watched, address books and letters are examined, telephones are tapped, and people are cross-questioned for hours on end about the names and habits of their friends and acquaintances.

Soon after I discovered my condition I began to realise that there are "queers" in all walks of life. Homosexuality is a great leveller, embracing the highest and the lowest in every land. Just as there are butchers and bakers and candlestick-makers who are "queer", so there are distinguished homosexuals whose lives, unless they are uncovered, remain private. Many are valuable members of the community, which frequently rewards them for their services.

Most homosexuals know a great many people. We are drawn together by suppression and persecution. I have met many hundreds of "queers". Some were lawyers, others journalists, financiers, bankers, doctors, engineers, chemists, labourers, waiters, and shop assistants. I have met police constables and a Scotland Yard detective who were homosexual. There were also people in the antique trade, the furnishing industry, commercial photography, the theatre, heavy industry, and the armed services.

I have met many "queer" authors whose books are best-sellers and probably on your shelves. Many of our finest actors and a great many Hollywood "heart-throbs" are strictly homosexual, including several favourite "pin-up" youngsters adored by teenage fans. The arts have always attracted homosexuals because artistic people are tolerant of such tendencies, and a creative calling sometimes acts as a substitute for having children. But of course *most* homosexuals work in very ordinary jobs and have nothing to do with the arts.

It is wrong to consider us "soft". Many boxers are homosexual. During the last war I met "queers" in all ranks from private to general. One of the bravest was a Battle of Britain fighter pilot who won his D.F.C. and Bar shooting down German 'planes over England. Twice he baled out of blazing Spitfires. Once his parachute landed him in a greenhouse. Twice the King congratulated him. Eventually he became a group-captain, although he had started his Royal Air Force career as an aircraftman. He was a highly emotional man, but he willed himself to do everything his companions did. He shot down more enemy planes than most of them, was a likeable and highly efficient fellow, and he really loved the R.A.F. So his companions accepted him readily, and regarded him with affection. He commanded a squadron of tough Polish fighters, among the best and most reckless of airmen. Most of the leading pilots who met him suspected or knew that he was homosexual, but no-one minded. But after the war, when so many of his comrades had gone, and life was less exciting, he was overcome by loneliness and an unjustified feeling that he had failed in his duty, when so many others had been killed. So he took a revolver and shot himself through the head. It was then that his "normal" friends, famous air aces of the R.A.F., asked the Air Ministry for permission to take the body and bury him in a tiny war cemetery near a famous fighter station, next to his comrades killed in action.

I am proud to have known him. He was one of the flying "few" who helped to save Britain in those dark days at the beginning of the 1939 war. But he was not the only "queer" hero I have met. Another was a V.C., who is still very much alive. He went through all the horrors of the Somme and Passchendaele and Ypres, and won his coveted decoration for leading a bayonet charge. A few years ago he went to Buckingham Palace to parade with other V.C.s before the Queen. Jokingly, he said to me before he went to the Palace, "Anyway, there'll be at least two queens there!"

In revealing some of the names of famous homosexuals of the past, I don't seek to glorify them, or our condition. I merely wish to show that homosexuals are not necessarily the maladjusted so-called "filthy perverts" condemned by ignorant opinion, and that if the advice of our enemies—that we should all be shot, or deported, or locked up—had been carried out, the world would have suffered as a result. No-one knows the names of all the homosexuals in history—from Michelangelo to Rudolph Valentino (ironically known as "the great lover")—who have made a success of their lives. But there is no doubt about some, for they have left behind evidence.

I personally knew two famous, popular homosexuals of our own time who were rightly admired by millions. I refer to Ivor Novello and Gilbert Harding.

Ivor Novello, handsome idol of theatregoers and one of the most popular men in Britain, was well known as a homosexual. No-one minded. But he thought, probably wrongly, that the prosecution which sent him to prison for a war-time petrol rationing offence was really brought because he was "queer". He went to jail believing the authorities had been determined to "get him", but that being unable to prove a homosexual charge, they found another. There is no doubt that prison hastened his death. He was never quite the same man again. When he died, the whole nation mourned. Thousands flocked to his cremation service. Men and women wept, unashamed.

Ivor was one of the most moral people I have met. He behaved decently and generously, and I doubt if he hurt anyone. He certainly tried not to. No-one could call his life "dirty" or "perverted", it was open and kindly. Knowing he could not be other than homosexual he determined to live decently, and never to offend people. He succeeded admirably.

He once said to me, "For many people it's hell being 'queer'. People say, 'Look, there goes Ivor Novello; he's rich and popular, isn't he lucky?' But I've had to work hard for it, and if I was indiscreet or foolish I could throw it all away with a single mistake. It's much more difficult for someone in the public eye. One must act all the time, pretending to be something you're not."

It was even more difficult for Gilbert Harding, who was a more complex character. Once he became well known he found life surprisingly complicated, and he crept deeper and deeper into his shell. His most important characteristic—homosexuality—had to be hidden from the public. He was always frightened of being "discovered" and of falling from public favour, not for his own sake, but because he wanted to go on helping other people. He had to be doubly careful what he said and how he behaved, which was a great strain for someone who was naturally outspoken, often sharp-tempered, and no hypocrite. Yet he never hid the truth from his more intimate friends. And in spite of his obvious—and very human—faults he was (as all his friends know) a really good man. Many thousands of people have reason to think of him with gratitude. And I believe the general public liked him for what he was. They saw a mixed-up, emotional, colourful, intelligent person, obviously fighting against illness, alcoholism, and the moody unhappiness which many homosexuals experience—and they admired him because he fought for what he believed was right.

Gilbert controlled his homosexual tendencies through his strong religious faith. It was no accident that he so often claimed he was a Roman Catholic. It was the sure shield which he had discovered, rather late in life, to help him with his condition. And the result was that although he often got drunk, and sometimes grew abusive, and was always extremely sorry next day, he managed to curb and control his homosexual desires, and live a celibate life. He felt he *had* to. People had made him into what he jokingly called a "telephoney"—and he didn't want to let either them or himself down. It was a responsibility, being a public figure, but the alternative was the gutter. As he once said to me, "I don't want to go back to the workhouse. People expect an awful lot of me, but I do try to lead a decent life, most of the time."

Those who knew him well, especially the priests and churchmen and intimate friends, have testified to the inherent *goodness* in Gilbert's life. It must have been difficult for such a moody, introspective, and emotionally disturbed man to be so often charming and kind and companionable. But he was, very often.

It is certainly not true, as has been suggested, that he was impotent. I once candidly asked him about his sex life, and he told me that he controlled his homosexual desires because he did not want to sin against God. Chastity, he believed, was an ideal for all of us who are unmarried. But how many of us can practise it, and if we do, are we likely to become as thwarted and lonely as Gilbert was?

He was certainly a surprising person. I was once in a pub with him when he was recognised by a crowd of Cockney trippers.

"Hullo, Gilbert!" they shouted across the room. "What's my line?" And they started dancing around, making faces.

Gilbert, trying to tell a story—he was always telling stories—suddenly grew pompous, climbed off his high stool, and walked out, mumbling. So I went over to the party and said, "Now look what you've done. You should have left him alone."

They were apologetic. "Honest, guv'nor," said a man in shirt-sleeves and braces, "we didn't mean to upset him. We think he's a wonderful bloke. It's a pity there aren't a few more Gilbert Hardings around."

Later that day I told Gilbert what the man had said.

"Really?" he said, looking surprised. And then emotional tears suddenly welled up into his eyes. "I thought they were barbarians, which only goes to prove that you can never be quite sure about people, doesn't it?"

Most "queers" were delighted when it became generally known that Gilbert was homosexual. I think we were rather proud of him. He was, in spite of all his faults, greatly respected by the public, for whom he did a great deal of good, especially among poor and helpless people. But many reformers are, or have been, homosexual. It is a characteristic of many "queers" that they want to help other people and to see wrongs righted.

II

History is studded with the names of famous homosexuals. Julius Caesar was one,[1] and there is also evidence that Alexander the Great and Marlowe the playwright were "queer". Charles XII of Sweden and Frederick the Great of Prussia certainly were. And so were William Rufus, Edward II, and William III, while James I was notorious for the "queers" in his court, his favourite, Robert Carr, having reputedly escaped punishment for murder by threatening to reveal his relations with the King.

The poet Tennyson was greatly influenced by his affection for a young man, and his "In Memoriam" poem to his friend provoked censure from *The Times*. The composer Tchaikovsky had strong homosexual tendencies and was actually in love with a girl and her brother at the same time.[2] To say that Tennyson and Tchaikovsky enriched humanity is an understatement. Like the homosexual actor David Garrick, they brought much beauty into an often drab world.

Many famous soldiers and statesmen have been "queer". General Gordon escaped from his homosexual instincts by becoming a tough, military father-figure. So did Field-Marshal Lord Kitchener, although he did not bother to be so discreet.

Kitchener of Khartoum, or "K" as he was known to the nation, typified the spirit that dominated the British Empire. At the outbreak of the 1914 war he was probably the most popular Englishman alive. The hero of Khartoum and the South African War, he virtually created the volunteer army which set the pattern for eventual victory. When he was drowned in *H.M.S. Hampshire* in June 1916 the whole Empire was stunned. King George V

[1] The Roman Senator Curio called Caesar "Every woman's man and every man's woman".

[2] Tchaikovsky's brother and his nephew were also homosexuals.

ordered all service officers to wear mourning bands. The King, the Queen, both Houses of Parliament, and the leaders of the nation went in solemn procession to St. Paul's to honour his memory.

Yet Kitchener was a practising homosexual and many people knew it. Queen Victoria once said, "They say he dislikes women, but I can only say he was very nice to me." To most people he was a stern, relentless disciplinarian. But behind the mask there was another Kitchener. And there are several men still living who intimately know the truth, and have never concealed it.

There is of course no evidence that homosexuality is increasing. The indications are that the percentage figures remain almost constant. It is now more widely discussed, and the subject is no longer "unmentionable", although there is still a great deal of ignorance about it. But our percentage in Britain is probably no higher than in the so-called "moral" Victorian days, when the subject (and all other sexual subjects) was taboo and such things were not fully reported by the Press. It would have been impossible for this book to have been published in the Victorian era.

Homosexuality was an important feature of life in fifth-century Athens, in late Elizabethan and Jacobean England, Renaissance Italy, and in the vigorously creative Germany of the nineteen-twenties. When revolutions occur, toleration ceases; "purity" campaigns are started which condemn all forms of free expression; drinking, dancing, the pursuits of pleasure and homosexuality are ready targets. So it is not surprising to note that just as Cromwell's government led Puritan reforms against these so-called "sins", so they are now condemned in Western Germany, Franco's Spain, and Nasser's Egypt. And in France, General de Gaulle's régime started in 1960 a great drive against homosexuals, turning them out of Paris cafés and bars, closing meeting places, while at the same time condemning what was called "excessive drinking" on the part of the population.

Other noted homosexuals of history have included T. E. Lawrence, the brave, uncrowned "King of Arabia",[1] the poet Gray (who wrote the famous "Elegy in a Country Churchyard"), the poet A. E. Housman of "Shropshire Lad" fame, and the great novelist Joseph Conrad.

The popular novelist Sir Hugh Walpole was also a practising homosexual. But it must not be thought that "queerness" is exclusive to the arts. For every Hugh Walpole there are many thousands of ordinary labourers or lorry drivers or salesmen who are also homosexual, but not necessarily artistic.

Leslie Hore-Belisha, War Minister at the beginning of the 1939 war, was unpopular at the War Office because he upset the "brass hats", tried to override the Generals, and sought reforms which aimed at improving the lot of the private soldier. A whispering campaign rumoured that he had homosexual tendencies. Then Hitler's radio actually named him as a homosexual. He was eventually forced to resign, and it was not until long after the war that his achievements were recognised and he was made a peer. The public regarded him—like Gilbert Harding—as the champion of the man in the street. The truth will probably never be revealed.

It is remarkable how many famous men have been homosexual, yet unknown as such to the general public. I once knew an eminent K.C. who entertained well. Cabinet ministers, clerks, students, lawyers, actors, foreign visitors, all met at his well-loaded table. Nearly all were homosexual. I don't remember seeing a woman at his flat. But the level of conversation was always high, and there I met famous scientists and doctors and well-known personalities. Our host, a witty, talented Irishman, who loved his wine almost as much as the companionship of his fellows, was warm-hearted and generous. As a conversationalist he had few equals. Today he would, if he were still with us, make an ideal television personality. I sometimes wonder what happened when he died, because his bedroom walls were lined with at least two hundred framed photographs of famous homosexuals whom he

[1] This has been disputed, although Lawrence indicated his tendencies quite clearly in his writings. The trouble is that he was a notorious liar.

had known during a long life—pillars of the Church, diplomats, judges, lawyers, service officers, and business men. Scotland Yard would have been surprised to see so many wigs on so many homosexual heads.

Another well-known homosexual of recent years was Sir Edward Marsh, for many years private secretary to Sir Winston Churchill, patron of the arts, and the man who could claim to have discovered the poet Rupert Brooke. Although I met Sir Edward only once, fleetingly at a theatre (where he wore a cape with red silk lining which in those days seemed rather exotic), he had innumerable friends and was the centre of a large homosexual artistic colony.

The actor Ernest Thesiger was another very successful homosexual. He was not only a brilliant actor but was also an expert at painting and needlework. He used to visit the late Queen Mary at Buckingham Palace, and later at Marlborough House, where they sat together doing fine needlework. There is evidence that Queen Mary accepted homosexuals, although it is unlikely that the subject was ever mentioned.

III

The history and literature of ancient Greece shows that homosexuality thrived among a virile, warlike people who fully accepted it as a noble form of love. They linked it with courage, devotion, and athletic prowess. Plutarch pointed out that love of youths was common in the greatest and most warlike of nations; Plato said that an army of lovers and their beloveds could win the world.

In the great days of the Roman Empire the poets glorified homosexual love. Catallus wrote a love lyric to a young man whose "honeysweet lips" he wished to kiss; Virgil, Horace, and Tibullus wrote in praise of the love of youths; Petronius considered it equal to the love of women.

The first great enemy of the "queer" tradition was the Hebrew faith—in spite of earlier approval. Some seven centuries before the birth of Christ, a Hebrew campaign against homosexuals was started in Palestine, on the grounds that it was a "foreign" custom. Christianity inherited this attitude from the Hebrews. The taboo against sex, even heterosexual sex for the procreation of children, had started. Fornication was held to be a "sin", became unmentionable, and was practised in the dark. By the middle ages, homosexuals were regarded as sorcerers and were in many countries burned at the stake. Their practices were considered "unclean", or "the infamous crimes against nature" or "unnatural and lascivious acts" or "the detestable and abominable crime". In England, homosexuality was known as "the French sin" or "the German sin". In Germany and France it was regarded as a wholly English crime. The words "abominable crime" still stand on the statute books of nearly all the States of the United States of America.

It was not until the revival of learning in Europe that a more enlightened interest in the subject was displayed by intelligent men. Leonardo da Vinci was stated to have homosexual relationships and Michelangelo sent love sonnets to a young man. With the introduction of the Napoleonic Code into International Law, the measure of tolerance was increased. This law stated that certain acts were criminal, but it did not list homosexuality as a crime, and the old Hebrew beliefs were at last checked.

The "Crime of Sodom and Gomorrah", it has been called, but there is no evidence in the earlier texts of the Bible that it was really homosexuality that was the so-called "crime" of the people of those cities. It is extremely likely that this is a myth. But many of the people who now oppose reform, and are strong opponents of homosexuals, claim they do so on religious grounds. The Bible, they say, calls homosexuality "an unnatural vice". If you are one of these people, perhaps you will consider the story of David and Jonathan as it starts in the first book of Samuel, Chapter 18:

> And it came to pass, when he had made an end of speaking unto Saul, that the soul of Jonathan was knit with the soul of David, and Jonathan loved him as his own soul. And Saul took him that

day, and would let him go no more home to his father's house. Then Jonathan . . . stripped himself of the robe that was upon him, and gave it to David, and his garments, even to his sword, and to his bow, and to his guide.

Later, in I Samuel 20, 37, come the words:

And when the lad was come to the place of the arrow which Jonathan had shot, Jonathan called after the lad, and said, Is not the arrow beyond thee? And Jonathan cried after the lad, Make speed, haste, stay not. And Jonathan's lad gathered up the arrows, and came to his master. But the lad knew not anything: only Jonathan and David knew the matter. And Jonathan gave his artillery unto his lad, and said unto him, Go, carry them to the city. And as soon as the lad was gone, David arose out of a place toward the South, and fell on his face to the ground, and bowed himself three times: and they kissed one another, and wept one with another, until David exceeded.

Most people consider the story of David and Jonathan, although completely homosexual, to be one of the most beautiful in the world. Consider also some of the names of later times who are known to have had at least homosexual leanings; such outstanding military geniuses as Alexander the Great and Julius Caesar, already noted; the Greek philosophers Socrates and Plato; Sapho, the poetess; Pindar, whose odes inspired mankind; Marlowe and Shakespeare and Francis Bacon among many great Elizabethans; Leonardo da Vinci, Michelangelo, and Cellini among the giants of the Renaissance; Tchaikovsky and Nijinsky among the Russians; Rimbaud, Verlaine, Baudelaire, Marcel Proust, and André Gide among the French writers; Goethe, Wagner, and Winkelmann among the Germans; the American Walt Whitman, who revolutionised poetry; Byron, Shelley, Oscar Wilde, Tennyson, and Gray among the English poets; Rosa Bonheur, the painter; and so many more whose names we can only guess, that any list must appear inadequate.[1]

There may be doubt about some of these names, but very little. Controversy has raged throughout the years over Shakespeare.

[1] These names have all appeared in other books dealing with homosexuals.

Homosexuals say he was, other people say he wasn't. There is evidence of homosexuality in several of his plays, and in his sonnets. But the venerable Walt Whitman, the bearded sage of Camden, makes his homosexuality quite evident throughout his poems. Few scholars are so greatly admired in the United States, where the laws against homosexuality are harsh.

As for Christopher Marlowe, he escaped execution for gross homosexual offences only when he was murdered in a public-house brawl.

The great Danish writer Hans Christian Andersen was a homosexual, and the opening lines of his autobiography cheerfully sum up his philosophy:

> My life is a lovely story, happy and full of incident. If, when I was a boy, a Good Fairy had met me and said, "Choose now thy course through life . . ." my fate could not, even then, have been directed more happily, more prudently, or better. The history of my life will say to the world what it says to me—there is a loving God, who directs all things for the best.

Recently, the poet Stephen Spender described in his autobiography the passing passion he developed at Oxford for a rather touching "hearty" friend, whom he painfully befriended, trying to share his sporting and mechanical interests, and going on a long walking tour with him.

"I only succeeded in embarrassing and boring him, and I bored even myself with the false relationship I had fabricated between us," says Spender. Eventually he felt he must precipitate a crisis, so he conversed with the youth and explained his feelings. When he had finished the other man looked up with a dazed expression and said naïvely: "Do you know, old son, this is the first time you've ever talked with me that I haven't been completely bored?"

The subject is a popular one with writers. In fact, *The Satyricon* of Petronius, which is believed to be the oldest existing novel in the world, is a homosexual story, although the events described, in the Roman Empire of the time, are rather sordid.

IV

There is perhaps some evidence of a growing—but slow—change in public opinion in Britain. The old "Soldiers in Skirts" revues are no longer there to be laughed at, and "Pansies" are not considered such screamingly funny jokes as they were in the nineteen-twenties or thirties; our problems are now discussed with increasing intelligence; people are at last starting to look around, to recognise that the average homosexual is a steady, conscientious worker and certainly not "a bad security risk"; his desire for perfection in detail, his acknowledged good taste, his willingness to work loyally for long hours, all help to make him a good administrator or employee. You will find many homosexuals in the Civil Service and in clerical jobs.

Yet too many people still remain mildly shocked by us. Nothing is taught in schools about our condition, and to the majority the subject remains "not quite nice". Therefore many of us cling together in a kind of hurt, misunderstood society. And some glory in the fact that they are "different" and "not as others", which is mentally unhealthy.

The tragedy of homosexuality is that while in groups we are usually bright, amusing people, we are often quite different when alone. Many of us, in our private lives, behind our front doors, in our small flats or bachelor rooms, are often introspective, unhappy, lonely people. Some of us, especially when we are older, lead sad, frustrated lives. Condemned by society, sometimes persecuted by police "drives", and always in danger of being misunderstood, we struggle to lead ordinary, decent lives. But in Britain the law and public apathy says that our desires and hopes are sinful and criminal. We may not share affections which to us seem perfectly normal, we must hide our feelings and learn to appreciate that we are outcasts in a so-called age of freedom. Freedom from fear is one of the rights of man, but it does not apply to homosexuals.

A person's interests and appearance have no bearing at all on his sexual characteristics. A women's dress designer may have a very powerful sex-drive, while a prize-fighter may not. A man may be small boned and slim and never have a single hair on his chest, and yet be completely male. But because to be "queer" is regarded by many as being "perverted" or "unclean", some of us go to extraordinary lengths to hide the truth, suppressing our real feelings, adopting extremely masculine manners and dress, anything to avoid facing the facts and come out into the open as we really are. This guilt complex has been forced on us for so long that it is taken for granted in Britain that all homosexuals are the natural enemies of the police, who are out to catch them. Thus, a very unsocial attitude towards the forces of law and order is common among homosexuals in Britain. But a single man against the law and public opinion can appear to face very unequal odds. And some of us think this a strange Christian society, which persecutes a minority of at least a million useful citizens.

The fact that Michelangelo and Tchaikovsky and Marlowe and Bacon (and possibly Shakespeare) were homosexual, and the knowledge that many successful men of today are "queer", doesn't really affect us more ordinary people or alter the pattern of our lives, except to supply the incentive which might be missing if we did not know that homosexuality need never prevent a man from reaching the heights in whatever profession or work he chooses.

In Britain our national newspapers give prominence to homosexual law cases involving well-known people. But every week hundreds of local newspapers report similar cases about relatively unknown "queers" who might be your neighbours, and often are. It should be remembered that for every case before the courts, there are many dozens of homosexual couples leading decent lives, helping one another, in defiance of the law.

Many older men find happiness with younger men, and I will take my own life as an example. I have already explained that I lived with another man for twenty-two years. He was a few years older than I, and when he died I thought that the best part of my life was over. No doubt I felt exactly the same as you would if, after nearly a quarter of a century of marriage, your partner—whom you loved deeply—died very suddenly and tragically. It would take you a long time to recover from the shock, as it did me. But time is a sure, if a slow, healer. And after a number of years I met someone else, a young man in his early twenties. And ever since then, for a considerable time now, we have been what homosexuals call an "affair". In other words, we have been "married" in a strong, romantic, and we believe, rewarding partnership.

For my part, I have been able to help him considerably, both with advice, and by introducing him to people he might not otherwise easily have met, and in aiding him to gain the career which was his ambition. But more important has been the affection and companionship and pleasure which he has given me in return. To say that I have been granted a new lease of life is an understatement; I have been introduced again to living. And ours are full lives in every way, based on trust and hope and devotion.

It has been like this for several years now, and it is no more likely to end than any marriage. The difference in our ages does not adversely affect our relationship. No doubt I make him feel older; certainly he makes me feel younger. When we are parted it is exactly the same for me as it must be for you when your wife or husband is away.

I suppose that one day it will end, but I do not fear the ending, any more than a man will fear losing his wife or a woman dreads losing her husband. There must, at some time, be an end to everything. But meanwhile we live decent, moral lives; we are not promiscuous, we are rather proud of our success in overcoming so many obstacles to happiness, and if in public we must hide our true feelings—simply because the average person wouldn't understand or accept our love—there are plenty of moments when he can show our affection.

Having long since adjusted myself to a homosexual way of life, being certain that I am incapable of any other way of living, I have no feeling of guilt. A few years ago, I think my friend felt guilty about being "queer". Many people he knew were promiscuous, with what I can only describe as a low-life outlook on homosexuality. But recently I have detected a decrease in his guilt complex. He is very happy in his job, now that he is doing what he wants; he has grown stronger and more sure of himself; and because our relationship has been accepted by his parents and is envied by most of his many friends, the feeling of guilt has almost gone.

Homosexuals are usually introspective people. I have examined my behaviour and our relationship many times during the last few years. Sometimes I have doubted if I am good for him, or if our relationship—outside the law from our first night together—can survive the prejudice and ignorance ranged against us. But it has survived, so far. And I now believe in my heart that our partnership, which has to date succeeded so admirably, cannot be wrong when it does so much good to two lives.

I am reminded of the man who recently said, "What does Lord Hailsham mean by 'promiscuous'? My friend and I have been together for thirty-five years." And to quote another—"I'm quite happy with my home and my friend—in fact a good deal happier than any of the marriages my two sisters and two brothers have made."

Gilbert Harding told me he would have liked to live with another man. "But how could I?" he said. "What would people think? I must live alone, and lump it, and pretend I prefer it that way."

Until legal persecution of homosexuals ceases in Britain, there will always be people as unhappy and guilt-ridden as Gilbert was. Why shouldn't he have lived with another man, if it would have helped him?

CHAPTER 3

Where We Meet

I

BEING social outcasts, many homosexuals tend to gather together, usually in pubs and clubs and coffee bars. In Britain—unlike many other countries—we are not allowed official meeting places. But in nearly every city and large town there is at least one unofficial place where many of us gather. We are brought together by the feeling of being outcasts and of being misunderstood. We wish to form friendships, and to meet others like us.

London has many bars and private clubs which are almost exclusively homosexual. In Birmingham there are two pubs. Glasgow has a club with several hundred members, and a big hotel and restaurant are also used. Aberdeen has more than one meeting place. Nottingham has a world-famous rendezvous, Portsmouth has several, Plymouth three, Leeds two, Bath two, and Bristol two. Groups meet every week-end at two hotels near Edinburgh, and later return to the city. Blackpool has two well-known meeting places, and Brighton has three clubs and two bars that are mainly "queer". With young people drinking less, there are also coffee bars in some towns where the local "queer" colony meets.

According to the Wolfenden Report, the cities of London,

Birmingham, and Portsmouth supply the largest number of homosexuals for English courts. But "queers" tend to migrate to the large cities, and as one of us has put it, "The people one sees around London are usually the more promiscuous ones. There are many more 'queers' who lead quiet lives with a chosen friend."

Few women go to the places which are mostly exclusively "queer". Sometimes the police know and watch the bars and coffee bars, and sometimes they warn the landlord or owner that his customers are "undesirables" and must not be served. The police seldom say who considers them undesirable, but it is usually the chief constable or a watch committee. If the "queers" are thrown out they move on to another place. But often the police let the colony stay, no doubt believing they are safer together than spread out over the town. It depends mainly on whether the chief constable is tolerant or intolerant.

One Brighton club has a world-wide membership of several thousands of homosexuals, and in the summer it is often crowded out. So is the inn in an unlikely back street in a Staffordshire town, which has for many years been one of the most famous meeting places in the Midlands. Homosexuals drive for miles at week-ends to drink and meet. But if you imagine these places are "dens of vice" or "sinks of iniquity" you are sadly mistaken. Even with several hundred homosexuals crowded into a bar or club, the majority are very well behaved. There are of course exceptions among all types of behaviour, but very few behave badly in these gatherings. Bad behaviour is not tolerated by the majority, nor is it desired.

There are no more "pick-ups" at these places than among men and women in any other bar or club or coffee bar. Certainly, the many homosexual bars and clubs I have visited are much less immoral, and are much less degrading, than the "normal" strip-tease clubs and honky-tonk dives of Soho, where men go to find loose women or gain sexual excitement with prostitutes.

Perhaps the most famous English homosexual meeting place of recent years was *The Running Horse* pub in Shepherd Market, off

Piccadilly, London. It is now a restaurant, but for many years before the 1939 war its famous long bar was packed nightly with as many as two or three hundred homosexuals.

Affectionately known as "the Horse" or "the Mare", it attracted men of all classes and income groups, and its reputation was international. Homosexual visitors from America, Holland, Germany, France, Italy—all crowded to *The Running Horse*. I have seen royalty there—a prince who shall be nameless—mixing with peers, clerks, actors, shop assistants, business men, soldiers, sailors; in fact a complete cross section of the male population of the metropolis. Homosexuals seldom observe any barriers or feelings of class distinction. After all, we are all in the same boat, and the feeling of being unwanted is common in varying degrees to all of us in Britain.

The fame of *The Running Horse* died hard. Only last year a German visitor asked me where it was. Yet it has been closed for some twenty years. Meanwhile, many other meeting places have come and gone. One popular London rendezvous, famous for nearly half a century, was the Long Bar of the Trocadero Restaurant in Shaftesbury Avenue. This was strictly for men only, and here, before and during and between two great wars, hundreds of thousands of men met to drink together, a very large percentage of whom were homosexual.

The famous promenade at the Empire Theatre, Leicester Square, although generally considered to be the haunt of "the ladies of the town" when that theatre was a music hall, was actually closed down because it became "queer". At another time the Monico Bar in Shaftesbury Avenue was a favourite meeting place. And in 1936, London's homosexuals unexpectedly chose a bar in the Regent Palace Hotel as a rendezvous. No doubt the management was surprised. But tastes change, and the colony soon moved elsewhere.

A public house or bar which claims homosexual attention finds its profits soaring, but they drop suddenly when the police disperse the "undesirable patrons", or warn the management. Sometimes a favourite barmaid attracts a group, and then everyone flocks to a hitherto neglected pub in Earls Court or Chelsea or Kensington, and for a while business booms there. The casual customer, walking in for a beer, might be surprised to see so many men together, but he will certainly observe no bad behaviour.

As one "queer" put it, "I once took a normal friend of mine there, who said it might be the National Liberal Club. Everyone was so good mannered and quiet. He said he wouldn't have suspected a single one of the people there."

Unfortunately, this doesn't stop the police from persecuting us, and magistrates usually support them. When a Soho public house was raided by police in 1953 there were 137 customers in the house, nearly all men. Of these the police said 91 were homosexual, but that "only 22 had been convicted". Evidence was given that the house had always been perfectly well conducted, but this didn't in the least impress Mr John Maude, Q.C., the Bow Street magistrate, who promptly fined the landlord.

"This is a class of pest," said Mr Maude, "which infiltrates licensed houses like mosquitoes crawling through mosquito nets. When they are cleared out of one place they settle down somewhere else."

Where did Mr Maude expect us to settle? In the streets? Should homosexuals in Britain be denied the right to meet and drink in public houses? And should 91 out of 137 men be condemned as "pests" without having committed an offence?

Unfortunately this magistrate, like many others, was confusing the good with the bad. Although most homosexual activities take place in private, we have to face the fact that a small minority of us behaves indiscreetly, and sometimes disgustingly, in public places.

In Britain, where we are driven underground, we have none of the restraining influences of so-called "normal" society, which keep most people from excesses. So a small minority of us is obsessed with sexual desire which they know to be forbidden by law. And the more this minority is driven on to the streets and into dark alleys, the more vicious and dangerous it becomes. Yet this minority should never be confused with the vast majority of homosexuals, who seek permanent partners and lead decent lives.

Most of us search for permanent love with our own kind, although society tells us it is wrong, illegal, "perverted", "filthy", and even laughable. But human instinct tells us it can be noble and worth while, and because it is natural to us, the majority try to make the best of what we are.

II

It is the minority which lets the side down, seeking elusive excitement in public places. In London these people create serious social problems, especially in railway stations, Turkish baths, in places like Piccadilly Circus, in crowds, at bathing places (like the Serpentine Lido), on open spaces (such as Hyde Park and Hampstead Heath), and, I regret to say, in public lavatories everywhere in Britain.

Homosexuals who frequent public lavatories to meet others are no doubt driven there because they are literally hounded out of other places, or because sometimes they do not know where else to go. But they do a great disservice to all "queers". They set back the hope of a change in the law. They maintain the medieval outlook on the problem, under which we homosexuals in Britain are forced to live. They corrupt themselves, and sometimes others, and they coarsen feelings which should not be cheap. The public finds it difficult to understand our problem, while the police continue to hound this minority. And the lavatory-mongers make things worse.

It is a criminal offence for a man to persistently solicit or importune in a public place for immoral purposes.[1] The maximum penalty for this offence is six months in prison on conviction on indictment. It is not easy to prove that a man has "persistently solicited", since a watch must have been kept over a fair period and his movements must have been carefully observed. The police evidence in such cases is important. Did the man stand around in the street making eyes at passing workmen? Did he run from

[1] The Vagrancy Act, 1834, Section 3.

corner to corner accosting young guardsmen? Or was he observed first in one lavatory in conversation with a stranger, then in another, and next in a third? And even then, was he merely begging?

Police evidence is, unfortunately, often accepted simply because it *is* police evidence, on the grounds that the police can't be wrong. And there is no doubt that *some* of the men sentenced for indecency in public places are wrongly sentenced.

Because society does not fully understand us, those who frequent these public places encourage the law against us. Few of the million or so male homosexuals now living in Britain are interested in vice or crime. We seek companionship with our own kind, and we require—like everyone else—sympathy and understanding. But if the law drives a million men underground then the weaker ones will meet wherever they can in search of the warmth of affection which should surely be denied no man or woman or animal.

There should be recognised clubs and meeting places where we are *encouraged* to go, and where—while we behave decently —we cannot be persecuted or thrown out on to the street.

In a town where an unsympathetic chief constable moves us out of pubs or clubs or coffee bars he is certainly moving some of us on to the streets. And if that isn't persecution, what is? You can hardly expect a million men to remain celibate just because the police tell them to be. And you can't put us all into jail for feeling something we can't help.

The public lavatories are constantly watched or patrolled by police "vice" squads whose job is to secure as many arrests as possible. In the often ill-lit side-street lavatories, it is no wonder that wrongful arrests are frequent.

I know a homosexual policeman who was asked to join the vice squad in a big city. His job was to help watch public conveniences at night, and to arrest men committing acts of indecency. The first man he saw was someone he had been drinking with at lunch time. The irony of the situation is obvious.

I know a police constable who was off duty, in plain clothes, enjoying a drink in a homosexual bar when two policemen on duty walked in. They looked embarrassed, because they were all friends. When they had gone, the policeman went to another homosexual bar, and the same two policemen came in, and saw him again. Next day the superintendent sent for him. "I don't mind your going to one 'queer' bar," he said, "but not *two* in the same evening. And remember, you're *never* off duty."

In 1953 a detective who had served for twenty years in the police force was sent to prison for indecency in a Turkish bath. The man had gone to the baths knowing full well that others had been arrested there by policemen who spied through peepholes in the wall.

Many Turkish baths in our cities and towns are frequented by the more promiscuous type of homosexual, as in most other countries. As a young man, serving in the Army overseas, I found it necessary to visit several baths or *hammams* in the Middle East. They were often the only places where one could properly wash off the accumulation of sand and sweat. I went there for no other reason, but I was surprised at the sexual behaviour I encountered. Since then I have talked to men I have met who regularly frequent baths in London and Paris and American cities, in order to find partners in quick sexual activity in the comparative privacy of the steam room. I have been told that the fact that privacy is usually incomplete heightens the excitement for those with exhibitionist tendencies. One of the most popular of these establishments is in the South-East district of London, well away from Mayfair.

III

What happens to a man who is arrested on a charge of "public indecency"?

A homosexual convicted of indecency in a lavatory has reported: "At the police station they were very nice, gave me cigarettes and called me by my Christian name. I was persuaded to rely on their sympathy. I was so green I didn't even realise I had been charged. This was on a Friday, and they said come back on Monday and they thought everything would be cleared up by then. On Monday, before I knew what was happening, I was whipped into court and given three months."

In one month in 1958 there were twenty-nine successful prosecutions against men for acts of indecency committed in a single London street convenience in Soho. The place was referred to by Mr Clyde Wilson, the Marlborough Street magistrate, as being "perhaps the most notorious place of its kind in London". It was almost permanently manned by plain-clothes policemen waiting to arrest offenders. Yet police who arrest men in such places sometimes do so on very slender evidence. In May 1959 Oxford magistrates dismissed two cases. The first concerned a man charged with importuning because when he entered the lavatory he "looked around". The second concerned a man who had "smiled at" another.

When a Kennington newspaper published a full report on a public lavatory where many arrests had been made, a man telephoned the editor saying, "Me and my mates don't like your story. And anyway—*where else is there to go?*"

The answer is that there should be official clubs to encourage such people to stay out of these places and behave decently.

"These unattended men's lavatories have been a source of trouble for many years all over London," said Mr Marcus Lipton, M.P. for Brixton. "They will continue to be sinks of iniquity until the government makes up its mind to carry out the recommendations of the Wolfenden Committee."

Sometimes even worse things happen. A bus conductor of twenty-eight who visited a lavatory in Mowbray Park, Sunderland, and was entirely innocent of any homosexual act, was attacked there by a drunken policeman off duty. As a result of the assault he was kept in hospital for six days. The policeman was charged with causing the man grievous bodily harm. In court he admitted, "I was in a disgusting condition—terribly drunk. I went to the park looking for homosexuals. I went there, I suppose, to have some fun at these fellows' expense." The judge sentenced him to three years' imprisonment.

In all cases where much is wrong, there are many ways of putting the matter right. Are so many public lavatories for men necessary in our towns? Most of them are unhygienic. Wouldn't prevention be better than prison? And wouldn't it be cheaper for the State, and less unseemly, to employ attendants in these places and to ensure that they are properly lit?

CHAPTER 4

Inside a Club

I

WHAT is it like inside one of our homosexual clubs? They vary greatly according to the country and the town, and no two are alike. In large cities like Amsterdam and Paris and Hamburg the homosexual bars are usually smart, sometimes luxurious, and occasionally expensive. And as in New York, Chicago, San Francisco, Washington, and other big American cities the "gay" clubs and bars cater for all classes of homosexuals. False concepts of class-consciousness and social position are swept away, the bars being frequented by all types of men, high and low, rich and poor. The only thing these men have in common is an incapacity to be sexually attracted to women, and even this is not entirely accurate because there will be, in such gatherings, a small percentage of bi-sexual men.

Let us visit one of these clubs, in the centre of London's so-called West End, and see what it is like. The entrance is through a main door at the side of a shop only a few hundred yards from Piccadilly Circus. A small, discreet notice outside gives us the name of the club and reminds us that it is for "members only". A passer-by or a casual visitor would think it exactly like any of the other hundreds of small drinking clubs in the Mayfair, Soho,

Kensington, or Victoria districts of the metropolis. But because it is for members only, strangers are unlikely to intrude.

We walk along a narrow passage, climb a flight of stairs, and enter the main room on the first floor. This is a tall, attractively decorated room whose windows are hung with expensive curtains. The taste is excellent if slightly theatrical. In this particular club the motif is Edwardian, and the huge cut-glass chandelier that hangs from the centre of the ceiling reflects the beauty of a past age. Under its light, the grey closely fitted carpet and the comfortable chairs and highly polished long bar look as if they might be part of a big European hotel. There is a washroom, a cloakroom, and an attendant to keep out intruders. If you are a member you may bring guests, but you must sign their names in the register, as in any other club in Britain.

The barman is a young man in a white jacket. You will probably discover, if you ask, that his last job was as a waiter at the Hotel Angleterre in Copenhagen or the Metropole at Brighton. He is one of the thousands of international hotel servants, probably Swiss or French, who understand all the vagaries of human nature, and are never surprised. He may or he may not be "queer", it isn't our concern, and it doesn't affect his job.

When we enter the club it is half-past eight, and it is unlikely that the room will fill up until nine or later. We buy two whiskies and sodas and we sit near the piano and look around. A middle-aged pianist is softly playing popular music, and we noticed that most of the other ten or twelve people in the room looked over when we came in, and eyed us up and down, as if summing us up. They will automatically be asking themselves, and answering, the following questions:

"Who is that?"

"Do I know him?"

"Have I ever met him before?"

"Is he one of us?"

A stranger in a club where most members know one another will perhaps excite some momentary interest. Naturally, if the visitor is very attractive, he will claim attention, as would an attractive woman or a pretty girl when entering an ordinary drinking club. But apart from the sexual interest, which does not necessarily predominate, the questions and thoughts which lie behind the quick scrutiny must be something like those which the ancient Christians posed when they watched strangers coming among them in the Roman Catacomb days.

"Is he one of us?"

The psychological reason for the question is the desire of all homosexuals not to be in a minority, not to be outcasts, but to be accepted. Weight of numbers gives us more confidence, and hope. That is why most of us like to be in, and to see, or to be part of, gatherings of homosexuals. It is the herd instinct, promoted by the persecution of our way of life. Alone, many of us feel unsure of ourselves because we know that the average person, sitting opposite in the bus or train or restaurant is not likely to be as we are. Actually, there is very little difference, but years of persecution, secrecy, and the shame which we have quite wrongly been made to feel, have created this feeling of apartness in our minds, making it difficult for us to behave like the majority.

The other men in the room are standing or sitting around, drinking and chatting. They might have come straight out of the R.A.C. in Pall Mall, or White's, or the Traveller's. It is unlikely that out of the ten or twelve men here, any one will look effeminate, but there may be one. The others are just ordinary-looking men of all ages, quietly talking. But there is a slight difference. Homosexual conversation in places like this is generally bright, and rather sharp-witted. It is likely in this West End club to be mainly about the theatre, or romantic experiences, or concerning the talkers themselves. "Queers" talk a good deal about themselves, but probably no more than anyone else. I have heard it said that homosexual conversation is usually more intelligent than heterosexual talk, but this is a ridiculous generalisation. In fact, it would be difficult, if not impossible, to judge any of these men as being homosexual if they were seen individually in a crowd.

As the American writer Donald Webster Corey has pointed out, the line of demarcation between friendship and sexual attraction is not always strongly delineated, and the classification of human beings according to the sex of their love-object is equally difficult. Appearances are deceptive.

It is only in the smarter, more prosperous part of the metropolis that you will find these clubs, and even then they are hard to discover. The East End of London, and the poorer district of any city, does not possess them. But in the less affluent areas homosexual liaisons in back streets and parks and Turkish baths and cinemas and public lavatories are quite frequent. Some public houses in the East End of London and in highly populated cities like Manchester or Liverpool or Birmingham are frequented by homosexuals of the extremely effeminate type. In many of these pubs there is singing, often led by female impersonators. Other customers mix freely with the "queers" and accept them.

But the club which we are visiting is more exclusive. To use the vernacular, it is "smart". We see not only the unaccompanied young man who is out for a good time, or hopes to meet someone, or regularly meets his friends here, but also the couples who have lived together for many years, in what can only be described as a "married" state.

II

There are a great many more of us "married" couples than you think. As I have already pointed out, very often a younger man is attracted by a much older man, or vice versa, and both can benefit enormously from such a liaison. The youth is guided by his senior, who in his turn gains new interests and a fresh outlook from the junior. It has been like this since the world began. In ancient Greece such companionships were regarded as more important than the "normal" married state. Warriors who fought side by side were often in love.[1] The Spartan and Theban armies were organised on this principle, lovers fighting together.

However, many "married" couples never go near these clubs, believing that they may lose their partners there. It is a reasonable

[1] For a good description of such a situation read Marie Renault's excellent novel *The Last of the Wine*.

attitude, because there is a percentage of promiscuous "queers" in these places. Some men use them as happy hunting grounds for sexual adventure. But in my experience most homosexuals regard the "married" state or "affair" as the ideal for all of us, even if at times it seems unobtainable.

While I know many queer "affairs" who have lived together for several years, there are others who do not wish to belong to any one person and are afraid of jealousies and scenes. These men spend many of their leisure hours in bars and clubs and meeting places where they can be sure of finding others like themselves. Many become exceedingly promiscuous, and seem contented only when seeking fresh sexual adventures, which seldom last long.

To appreciate how a homosexual feels in one of these clubs, and the temptations which surround him, imagine what you would feel if, as a so-called "normal" man, you went into a club full of women, but with no men present. No doubt some of the women would attract you. That is what a "queer" finds in these places. But these clubs and other meeting places are no more immoral than any other drinking clubs. Certainly they are not the "dens of vice" which they are sometimes supposed to be. Englishmen have conveniently forgotten that in the eighteenth century there were many homosexual brothels and clubs in London. One, the *White Swan*, was exposed in 1810 and seven men were put in the pillory in the Haymarket, where a huge mob behaved with savage brutality.

All kinds of people come to this little club, to talk and drink. We may meet friends—a middle-aged man who works in a bank, and his younger friend—a young man who hopes one day to write the play of the century—an American who works in Grosvenor Square—a visitor from the Midlands who has been given an introduction by his own club. The conversation is usually of a homosexual nature, which is admittedly a bad habit with us, growing out of repression and the fact that most of the time we have to hide our true instincts. The ballet is discussed, someone talks about a new revue, or the performance of a star in the latest play. Politics are very seldom mentioned, sport hardly ever. A casual observer might consider the conversation superficial. In many ways it is. No one desires to be intense or to argue or debate or try to solve the problems of the world. Here, the idea is to have an enjoyable, light-hearted time. Indeed, homosexuals in collective groups are often so entertaining that they attract the company of women of fashion and art, or those who find the average male dull by comparison.

You will observe that the men around you are well dressed. In such clubs the standard and quality of clothes is high. Most "queers" are concerned about their appearance, revealing the feminine side of their nature in a love of colour, carefully made suits, original designs, and a progressive attitude towards dress. Usually, they show good taste.

The chatter around us is light-hearted and casual. In such places one man is often introduced to another by his Christian name, ignoring the surname. The atmosphere is a great deal more friendly and informal than in so-called "normal" clubs. But in this kind of place you will find less permanent "affairs" than outside.

If you were ever to actually get inside one of these clubs, you would receive few surprises. I have seen men and women go into a "queer" bar by mistake, look around, realise that the assembly was almost entirely male—perhaps a hundred men standing and sitting and talking and drinking—and then, sooner or later, leave the bar. No doubt they thought there was something slightly strange or odd about the gathering. I have also seen stupid people who have entered bars frequented by homosexuals, in order to "laugh at the pansies". One woman I know took her house guests along, and almost the first person she saw, sitting up at the bar chatting to a good-looking young man, was her own adult son. I have no idea how she explained things to her guests. But I don't think she stayed to laugh.

CHAPTER 5

Prison for Homosexuals?

I

PRISON constantly threatens every one of us million male practising homosexuals in Britain. Yet there are more homosexual acts committed *inside* prisons than in the so-called "free" world outside. To us "queers" the world beyond the prison gates is not free, because we are always in danger of persecution.

Sending a "queer" to prison has been described as like locking up an alcoholic in a brewery. A young man recently sentenced for a homosexual offence was promptly seduced by one of the warders. And in 1960 two youths were convicted at Glamorgan for homosexual conduct which took place privately *in a prison cell.*

A senior prison officer from Dover has revealed the truth about homosexuality in prisons. "We talk about homosexuality in the outside world," he said, "but only those who work in the precincts of prisons know the danger."

Ex-prisoners report that homosexual practices are so common in jail that it is impossible to avoid putting "queers" together in cells, even when three men are together. Nor is the third man a real deterrent.

Yet judges and magistrates still send us to jail for being something we cannot help, and which all the medical science in the world cannot cure.

A young man recently sent to prison for a homosexual offence reported that the place was so full he had to share a cell with three others. And when at last he got more privacy a warder came and "made use of him" from time to time.

The sentence a homosexual receives if found guilty of an offence depends largely on the attitude of the judge or magistrate. It varies enormously in different courts. Some judges still belong to the "filthy-swine-should-be-horsewhipped" school. Others think all "queers" are corruptors of youth, which is a very common error. Sentences for the same offence vary even in the same court, and are often haphazard.

In May 1959 two young men pleaded guilty to three acts of sodomy in the course of a long friendship. They had been arrested because affectionate, private letters written by one to the other had gone astray and were handed to the police. There was no question of the letters being indecent. They were love letters. The judge said he appreciated that both men were of good character, had never been in trouble before, could not help their tendencies, had caused no affront to public decency, and that no corruption was possible. He then sentenced them to nine months imprisonment.

But that is not all. In the same court and on the same morning the same judge *bound over* a man who pleaded guilty to an act of sodomy in a public place.

In fact, sodomy is equally illegal if committed by a man with a woman, whether married or not, but this section of the law is very seldom applied. Medical authorities believe it is certainly no more common among homosexuals than among so-called "normal" men and women.

Some homosexuals are fortunate to appear before intelligent magistrates. One, in London, recently said, "It is obvious this poor man should be dealt with by the doctors. But the law clumsily makes no arrangement except committal for trial, so I must commit him to the Old Bailey."

Unfortunately, not all justice is so enlightened. And local newspapers are often unsympathetic. During a case of indecent assault at Hertfordshire Quarter Sessions the chairman sentenced the prisoner and then asked the Press not to publish the man's name because of the effect it might have on his elderly mother. One newspaper not only printed the chairman's request in full, but also published the man's name eight times.

So another homosexual went to prison, and eventually returned to a world which has still discovered no cure for him. Yet he was more fortunate than the twenty-three-year-old prisoner who recently hanged himself in his cell at Wormwood Scrubs because of his love for a fellow prisoner who had written to him that it was "finished between them".

What does a "queer" feel like when he comes out of jail? Has he been reformed, or punished, or licked into shape by his experience? Let journalist Peter Wildeblood supply the answer. After serving a sentence for his part in the Montagu case, he wrote, "I seek only to apply to my own life the rules which govern the lives of all good men; freedom to choose a partner and, when that partner is found, to live with him discreetly and faithfully. Discretion and fidelity are, however, made almost impossible by the present state of the law."

I count myself lucky. I am a practising homosexual, but I have not yet fallen out with the law. I try to behave discreetly and faithfully and I believe I have found the right partner. But as the law stands today I might be sent to prison at any moment. The police could simply set a trap for me and catch me in my own home.

Those one or two million of us who are unfortunate enough to be born different from the majority should remember what a homosexual wrote to Mr Montgomery Hyde, the Tory M.P. for North Belfast:

> God in Heaven only knows the fights I have put up against it. I am sure I am only one of many, and I have lost each time. It seems so utterly ridiculous for two men who wish to live together

in their own home to be classed as criminals and sex maniacs. I know men and women who have committed far worse acts than homosexuality, who look upon us as if we were murderers.

I know several "queers" who have been to prison. Most of them hated it, but of course it didn't and couldn't cure them. They came out feeling bitter against a society which had condemned them for being something they couldn't help, but jail hadn't altered their condition. You can't teach or discipline a man not to be a homosexual, any more than sending a deaf man to prison will make him hear. Homosexuality and deafness are both physical conditions, not vicious habits.

While in prison a friend of mine met another young prisoner with whom he fell in love. They now live together, and jokingly reflect that but for gaol they might not have met. But the strict enforcement of the law against "queers" usually brings misery, especially to innocent families and parents. Many relations have long known of their son's or brother's or even father's condition, and have felt powerless to help. Prison comes as a social and family disgrace.

If all the doctors and scientists in the world can't help us, how can prison warders, many of whom also have homosexual tendencies?

Donald J. West, whose book on the subject[1] is a frank and practical approach to the problem, points out that fiercely possessive relationships develop in restricted prison communities, leading to violent quarrels and jealousies.

In his book *Sex in Prison*, the American J. F. Fishman, an ex-Inspector of Prisons to the U.S. Government, explains how the impersonal discipline with no outlet for affection, the absence of women, enforced idleness, perpetual salacious talk, loss of self-respect and normal standards, all conspire to lead prisoners into homosexual habits. After repeated prison experience, a youth may soon lose all desire for women, and become orientated to homosexuality.

[1] *Homosexuality*, by Donald J. West (Penguin Books).

II

One reason why homosexuals are persecuted and sent to prison is the widespread belief that they are a menace to children. But the average homosexual is no more sexually interested in children than the average heterosexual. Most of us find no sexual attraction in children. But just as many "normal" men find girls of seventeen or eighteen or nineteen attractive, so are some homosexual men attracted by youths, who although they may be under twenty-one are nevertheless sexually mature. And it is by no means always the older man who makes the first advances; the youth often takes the initiative.

It is clear that only a minority of homosexuals or those who indulge in homosexual acts fall into the hands of the police or seek medical advice. Therefore, police records and evidence on homosexual behaviour are based mainly on the worst cases, for the more anti-social type of person is more likely to attract the attention of the police, except in the case of "witch-hunts", and mass investigations, when anyone may be roped in.

People from all walks of life go to prison for "queer" offences, whether committed in private or public, no matter how long ago. At York Assizes a recent big case involved a coal lorry mate, an accounts clerk, an apprentice fitter, a greaser, a shop manager, an agricultural engineer, a steelworker, an electrician, a 'bus conductor, and a storekeeper. None looked particularly effeminate. None had been in trouble before. None were "criminals" or of bad character, and all were grown-up men. But all were victims, as were their relatives and friends, of an out-of-date law. And only in Britain, the United States, certain Commonwealth countries, and Western Germany could they have been sent to jail.

In my experience the so-called "working classes" accept homosexuality with a shrug of the shoulders, having always lived with it. They have seen it around them, and privately they think it nothing unremarkable. Living close together, they understand it. The main enemy of us "queers" in Britain is the middle-class man or woman with a little education who prides himself or herself on being "superior" and "respectable" but is not always particularly moral.

Most women understand homosexuality, and accept it. But what happens to the people who say, "I'd like to see all the damned pansies castrated", and then find out that their own sons are inescapably homosexual? Do they blame themselves, or do they hope their sons will go to prison?

It is clear that for the individual who is sent to prison, segregation in an over-crowded jail serves only to encourage his homosexual practices. Confinement embitters the individual without reforming him, and helps to spread homosexual habits among men who might otherwise not indulge.

Judge Tudor Rees, the chairman at the 1953 annual magistrates' meeting of Surrey County, has said:

"In my view, except for the removal of the corrupting influence, prison is not the answer to the problem. To lock up in solitary confinement for eighteen hours out of twenty-four a man convicted of an unnatural offence is to do him far more harm than good. In the innumerable hours that he has to spend alone he quite naturally contemplates those very things that he ought to be encouraged to forget. I have had talks with governors and medical officers of prisons, and with probation officers and others, and I am sure that, instead of reforming the offender, a prison sentence aggravates the cause of the trouble, and so inevitably leads him into further mischief when he leaves prison."

No general guidance has ever been given by the Home Office to chief constables in Britain about the administration of the law against homosexual behaviour. The matter is therefore left to the individual attitude of chief constables, depending on their knowledge, ignorance, and bias. A homosexual might be persecuted in one town, but tolerated in another. The interpretation of the law in Britain is left to individuals who are not always qualified to know what they are dealing with—homosexual behaviour being wrongly regarded as a "crime", comparable to theft, blackmail, house-breaking, and robbery with violence.

Sometimes a whole group of men is prosecuted as a result of

a police "witch-hunt". In July 1954 twenty-eight men were taken before the Birmingham Assizes on charges of homosexuality. The judge spoke of "these disgusting practices which corrupt the life of the community", and passed prison sentences amounting to thirty-six years. The case was the result of one man giving the police an address book containing the names of 213 homosexuals whom he had known over a period of many years.

Suppose that each of those twenty-eight men had four relations, although in fact there must have been more. Thus, at least 112 other people were shamed and made miserable because of the judge's words. Their George, Fred, Harry, Bill—brother, son, nephew, uncle, even father—had been condemned by a judge for "disgusting practices" which came to light because of an address book. There was no evidence that anyone had been corrupted, or damaged, or injured, or hurt. But the law maintained that the men had, at various times, "offended against society", an expression which does not bear close examination.

What does it mean? Do people who make atom bombs "offend against society"? Is a man who sells armaments, or who by his actions helps to raise the cost of living, an offender against his neighbours? Is it really an offence against the people of Great Britain for two men to undress and get into bed together and make love in a private bedroom? And why is it *not* an offence for a married man to leave his wife and children and go off to bed with a girl he has met only twice before, with whom he intends to create a new family?

III

But let us return to the so-called "witch-hunts". What exactly happens when one of these secret investigations is started by the police?

According to the Wolfenden Report, "A man is questioned by the police about an offence under enquiry, and in the course of the interrogation admits having indulged in homosexual behaviour with men whom he names. These men are then confronted with the statement made by the first man, and, in turn, they make statements, involving further men. The process repeats itself until eventually a large number of men may be involved. The police sometimes take considerable trouble in following up alleged offences revealed in this way, and their enquiries often bring to light offences committed some years earlier."

The following three examples of what I call the "witch-hunt" danger were quoted in the Wolfenden Report:

(1)

A., aged 20, was being questioned by the police regarding other offences (not homosexual offences), and made a statement admitting acts of gross indecency with B., aged 32, some twelve or eighteen months earlier; in the course of his statement he also said that he had witnessed acts of mutual masturbation between B. and two youths of 17 some three years earlier. B. and the two youths were questioned by the police and made statements admitting the acts which A. had witnessed. Eventually B. and the two youths (by now young men of 20) were prosecuted in respect of these acts. The Chairman of Quarter Sessions, in discharging the younger men absolutely, expressed his disapproval of the proceedings against them.

(2)

X., a nineteen-year-old serviceman stationed in Egypt, who was apparently being questioned by the service police in connection with homosexual offences which had occurred at the Station at which he was serving, made a statement which included references to an offence which had occurred five years earlier between Y., a man of 47, and himself, in a cinema in his home town. Y. was in due course questioned by the police in this country, to whom X.'s statement had evidently been passed by the service police, and made a statement admitting this offence and a number of other offences over a period of years, including some with Z., a man of his own age, which had taken place some six or seven years previously. There had, so far as is known, been no offences between Y. and Z. for over six years, but Z. was charged with, and convicted of, an offence which had taken place six years previously. Z. was not charged with any other offences.

(3)

C., aged 45, was observed by the police to be associating with men younger than himself and his movements were watched. As a result of this observation it came to the notice of the police that he had, on a particular night, shared a single room, at the hotel where he was employed, with D., aged 21 years. D. was accordingly questioned by the police and admitted offences with C. on the night in question and other similar offences which had occurred a few nights previously.

C. was then questioned by the police, and admitted not only the offences with D., but also a number of other offences going back for some twenty years. Among the offences so admitted were acts of gross indecency committed some twelve or thirteen years earlier with E., then a youth of 17. There was no suggestion that any offences had been committed with or by E. during a period of at least ten years prior to the date at which C. was being questioned.

The police nevertheless questioned E., by now a man of 30, occupying a responsible position and happily married with two children. E. admitted that acts of mutual masturbation had taken place with C. over a period of seven months some thirteen years earlier. On the advice of the Director of Public Prosecutions, no proceedings were taken in respect of the offences between C. and E. owing to the lapse of time.

Reading these reports, are you surprised that many homosexuals refer to the police on these occasions as the *Gestapo*? There could be no more unpleasant association of ideas. Once the "witch-hunt" has been ordered, the net closes around men and boys of all ages, regardless of the fact that young people are more inclined to homosexuality than the old. A teen-aged boy is at the height of his sexual prowess. Often, he will indulge in homosexual practices, but when he grows older he will, in the majority of cases, not indulge further. He is homosexual only during this particular phase of his life. But the law makes no distinction.

During the year 1955 no less than 236 youths between seventeen and twenty-one were convicted of homosexual offences by the English courts.[1]

Of course *all* men found guilty of homosexual offences are not sent to prison by the English courts. In 1955 only thirty per cent of the persons found guilty were sent to prison; and in Scotland, during the same year, only thirty-seven per cent went to prison. The rest were discharged or bound over or put on probation or fined, and in the case of younger offenders were sent to Borstal, detention centres, approved schools, or attendance centres. Twelve per cent were absolutely or conditionally discharged; about three per cent were bound over; twenty-four per cent were put on probation; thirty per cent were fined.[2] But the number of men sent to prison on so-called "moral" grounds is still appallingly high, and the ignorance of those who administer the law is remarkable.

"This disgusting perversion should be stamped out," said a magistrate recently, sentencing two young men to prison.

Homosexuals are often wrongly referred to as "sexual perverts". But very few homosexuals are perverts. A sexual perversion is an emotional condition in which a person cannot find satisfaction in *normal* intercourse with a partner of the opposite sex. The pervert is an emotionally sick person and his deviation may take any one of several forms—exhibitionism, in which a man seems compelled to expose himself—sadism, which associates sex desire with the infliction of cruelty or violence—masochism, which craves suffering or humiliation, and fetishism, a condition in which sexual feelings are aroused by the sight or touch of some particular part of a woman's body or clothing. A man may be excited by women's feet, or gloves, or shoes, or raincoats.

All this has nothing to do with homosexuality, and people who put us into a category with sexual perverts are mistaken. As for

[1] Wolfenden Report, 1957. [2] ibid.

the magistrate who announced that homosexuality should be "stamped out", he might just as well have said that no more twins were to be born into the world.

The old taboos die hard. Several years ago I went to see Robert Morley in the play *Oscar Wilde.* In the interval an elderly man next to me said, "If I had a son like that, I'd have him publicly thrashed." I felt like telling him that I was "queer", as was at least a third of the audience. But I said nothing, and he sat there hating the rest of the play, while most people around him liked it.

No doubt he would say that homosexuality is increasing, but in fact there is no evidence at all that the percentage of homosexuals has increased. There are of course a great many more people in Britain now than, say, twenty years ago, and therefore more homosexuals, but homosexuality is not a contagious disease or a cult, so there is no reason why it should increase. And many of the official figures are misleading. For instance, between 1951 and 1956 the reported homosexual offences quadrupled in Victoria, New South Wales. In Sydney the increase was sixty-six per cent in four years, against an increase of only two and a half per cent for other incidents. The figures represent arrests made outside cinemas and in parks. And they led Mr Delaney, the New South Wales Police Commissioner to ask, "How many are carrying on behind closed doors?"

Mr Delaney's active personal dislike of homosexuals had caused a vigorous persecution, bringing to light more homosexual offences than the State had previously known. But there is no evidence that the percentage of "queers" is any higher in Australia than ten or twenty years ago. All that is proved is that Mr Delaney hates homosexuals and vigorously attacks them.

IV

Men arrested for public homosexual acts are often drunk, or have been drinking. In our loneliness, we "queers" sometimes turn to alcohol to strengthen a feeling of being accepted. But homosexuality and strong drink seldom mix well. A person with "queer" tendencies when under the influence of strong liquor often performs acts which his conscience would forbid when sober. But this is true of nearly everyone.

Gilbert Harding once admitted that nearly all the acts he was ashamed of had been committed when he had drunk too much. In his case they involved being rude to people, saying exactly what he thought, and sometimes being a nuisance. Next day he was always desperately sorry. But the practising homosexual (which Gilbert was *not*) when drunk often abandons his inhibitions and becomes a public pest. He discovers a courage he doesn't really possess, and flaunts his sense of inferiority in the face of public opinion. Then the police step in.

Homosexuals who have difficulty in controlling their desires should never drink to excess. But of course this applies to everyone who is adversely affected by alcohol.

People are no longer hanged, drawn, and quartered—as they once were—for stealing oranges. Isn't it time you stopped sending us adult men to prison for what you call "acts of gross indecency" in our own homes, while our sisters and cousins and aunts can do what they like? You don't send home-breakers to prison, although they cause infinitely more misery than we do. Adultery isn't punished by law. People aren't sent to jail for producing illegitimate children. Rightly or wrongly, we homosexuals think *these* are far greater crimes than living with the man one loves, while harming no one.

Mr John Gordon of the London *Sunday Express*, who apparently has a strong animus against homosexuals, reported the case of a Maidstone prisoner who committed suicide in his cell. He was doing two years for a homosexual offence. Another prisoner, giving evidence, said he and the homosexual visited one another in their cells in the evenings.

"Quite a home from home, isn't it?" said Mr Gordon in his column, disregarding the tragic end of a life.

Has it ever occurred to him that prison isn't the right place for homosexuals?

According to Sir John Wolfenden, his committee did not agree that "queers" should go to jail.

It is not enough to claim that the law has been the same for many years and therefore should not be changed. A little over a hundred years ago men were hanged for petty theft. The law was changed because juries refused to convict. It has been claimed that *all* English laws are many years behind public opinion. But there is still so much ignorance and prejudice in Britain about homosexuals that the Home Secretary is afraid of a change. And so, therefore, is the Government.

But if something isn't done to recognise our condition and help us, a million homosexuals will, sooner or later, *demand* reform. We are not an unimportant section of the community.

CHAPTER 6

In other Countries

I

EACH of us—no matter who we are—has moments in which folk of our own sex seem more interesting, more attractive, or may be simply easier in relationship than those of the opposite sex. On reflection, you will not be surprised when you realise that our particular condition knows no barriers of race or creed or country. It exists wherever there are men and women, as well as where there are animals. It is part of the natural pattern of life.

In most of the great cities of the world—Amsterdam, Paris, New York, Hamburg, Brussels, Chicago, Rome, Copenhagen, Vienna—homosexuals gather freely in private or public places, within the law. And in most cities outside Britain and America and Western Germany we "queers" are accepted as human beings and are not regarded as freaks. But the law varies in different countries. In Belgium, homosexual behaviour is not punishable and the homosexual sexual act is punishable only if it constitutes a public offence. In Denmark and Sweden and Spain, homosexual sexual behaviour between consenting partners is not punishable unless it involves abuse of the young or is an affront to public decency. In France the law is the same where consenting partners of over twenty-one are concerned, but there has been a drive against homosexuals, especially in Paris, since De Gaulle came to power. Italians do not punish homosexual behaviour as such. In Holland, homosexual acts between mutually consenting partners both of whom are over twenty-one, or both of whom are between sixteen and twenty-one, are not punishable unless public decency is affronted. In Norway, the law provides that an offender shall be prosecuted only if it is essential in the public interest.

An independent enquiry in Sweden has suggested that one per cent of all men in that country are homosexual and about four per cent have both homosexual and heterosexual impulses, but official sources in Sweden have later indicated that these figures are probably too low.[1]

The average homosexual has an easier, happier life abroad than in Britain. Many of my friends live in Italy or Denmark or Switzerland or North Africa, rather than face the risk of persecution here. Yet countries without our antiquated laws against homosexuals report no increase in numbers. Why then does anyone expect an increase here? Are we supposed to be less moral than foreigners?

Where there is no law against homosexuals as such, the crime problem is simpler, because no problem exists.

Amsterdam is famous for its homosexual night life, which is very morally conducted. Its bars and clubs stay open until late hours. Because of our laws, many thousands of English homosexuals visit the city every year, to mix freely with the Dutch. The authorities recognise that a great many "queers" live in Holland—as everywhere else—so in order to integrate them into the community they allow them their own, official clubs. These are well conducted and strictly controlled. The police were invited to the opening of one of Amsterdam's biggest "queer" clubs thirteen years ago, and they have never needed to go there since. The club provides intelligent literature, publishes a magazine, and encourages homosexuals to lead moral lives and feel "wanted" by the community—and not by the police. The harm-

[1] Wolfenden Report, 1957.

ful effects of isolation which many homosexuals feel in Britain do not affect our Dutch cousins.

Copenhagen has three "queer" clubs. On the rare occasions when the Danish police find a homosexual importuning or soliciting on the streets they put him into a car and take him to one of the clubs, where he can be with his own kind and not be a nuisance. Isn't this a more civilised approach than sending him to jail? And what is the result? Simply that there are very few homosexuals on the streets in Denmark. Can one say the same for Britain?

There are also clubs in Brussels, Stockholm, Oslo, Bremen, Frankfurt, Hamburg, and Basle. In the United States there is a social organisation for female homosexuals in San Francisco, and another for men in the same city, with branches in Denver, Los Angeles, and New York, while a second club in Los Angeles maintains education and research divisions to *help* homosexuals. In Britain today, as we shall see, hundreds of us go to prison every week, into crowded cells where there is no known cure for our condition.

Let me tell you a true story about what happened to a friend of mine on holiday in Copenhagen. One afternoon he was walking near Nyehaven when he unexpectedly met a young Danish sailor. They looked at one another, liked what they saw, and started talking. It has been so since the creation, all the laws in the world cannot keep lovers apart. They went back to my friend's hotel, he explained the circumstances to the porter (whom he knew would understand) and went upstairs. I will call my friend David, although that is not his name. The Dane was named Paul. Nearly everyone in Denmark speaks English.

Some two hours later the sailor prepared to go. David said that he would like, before they parted, to give him a present, something to be chosen in Copenhagen. Meanwhile, he asked, would he have a drink that evening? David had to go out with a Danish family he knew, but would Paul accept fifty kroner (about fifty shillings) in order to have a drink?

The sailor hesitated, so David reminded him that the Navy

didn't pay him overmuch, whereas he—David—was quite well off. Fifty kroner wasn't much. How about some English cigarettes as well, from the 'plane? Paul hesitated no longer, shook hands solemnly with David, and left.

My friend had a bath, put on a clean shirt and smart suit, and went out into the bright, crisp air of the city. But he had walked only a few yards when someone behind him said in English, "Excuse me," and he turned and saw a small, middle-aged blond man wearing a grey suit. All Danes seem to be blond.

"Excuse me," said the stranger, "are you English, and are you staying at the —— hotel?"

"Yes," said David.

"Then I wonder if you will kindly come to the police station with me. I am a police officer. It isn't far, only just along the road."

David says he was frightened. Thoughts of arrest, dishonour, even deportation, crowded into his mind. Being English, he at once felt guilty about the sailor and the afternoon. But he found the policeman pleasant company, and as they walked along they discussed the Tivoli Gardens, and the attractions of Copenhagen.

There were two uniformed police officers in the station. One, obviously the senior, rose from his desk, bowed, held out his hand, and waved David into a chair.

"May we please see your passport?" he asked, and when they had examined it he added, "Did you take a sailor into your hotel at about three o'clock this afternoon?"

"Yes," said David, his mouth uncomfortably dry.

"And did he demand any money?"

"Demand?"

"Did he ask for money? Did he suggest you should give him money?"

"No," said David, "certainly not. It wasn't at all like that. I suggested he might like to go out tonight—for a drink—I gave him fifty kroner. It was a present, a gift. In fact he didn't want to take it at first."

"I see," said the senior policeman, "and is that all you gave him?"

David remembered. "No, I also gave him some cigarettes. A tin of fifty English cigarettes. He was a very pleasant fellow. I wouldn't want to get him into trouble."

The policeman smiled, opened a drawer, brought out fifty kroner and the tin of cigarettes, and laid them on the desk.

"Thank you," he said, "we shall return them to him. We picked him up as he left the hotel. I am very sorry to have caused you this inconvenience, but we have to safeguard our visitors and make sure they are not intimidated. It is criminal to demand money on such occasions. The sailor was telling the truth, so all is well. We hope that you have a pleasant stay in Denmark, and that you will enjoy yourself." Smiling, the policeman shook David by the hand. They delivered him to his friends in a patrol car, and waved good-bye as they drove off.

II

What of homosexuals in the United States?

When Kinsey's famous report was published, the American nation was shocked to discover that more than a third of the male population had had some homosexual experience leading to orgasm, after adolescence; about half of the men who remain single until they are thirty-five have had some such experience; and about one-third of *all* males go through a three-year period at some time after the start of the adolescent period during which they have "at least incidental homosexual experience or reactions".

According to Kinsey, about ten per cent of the male population of the United States is "more or less exclusively homosexual" for at least a three-year period; eight per cent is exclusively homosexual for such a period; and four per cent exclusively so for their entire lives.

The great American public hastily repudiated these findings, which shocked them. An army of fact-finders, doctors, psychologists, and statisticians attempted to disprove Kinsey, but without success. The Kinsey team had worked thoroughly, and all the evidence indicates that if there was an error it is that there are in the United States more of us, and not fewer, than the Kinsey report claimed.

According to the American author Jess Stearns, *every sixth man* in the United States is a homosexual. Yet few people are so bitterly opposed to homosexual behaviour as Americans.

In 1950 a vicious crusade against homosexuals in the United States Government service was undertaken as part of a political campaign by the notorious Senator McCarthy. Starting as an attack upon the Truman administration, it soon extended to all government offices. Homosexuals, ignorantly described by McCarthy as "sex perverts", became the scapegoats in a fierce battle. Nearly a hundred homosexuals, whose private lives had been revealed by a series of witch-hunts, were suddenly dismissed from the State Department. They were loyal employees—many were experts in their field—but all were dismissed because they were charged with being homosexuals. Not with sexual behaviour between males, but with *being* homosexual. It was officially claimed that homosexuals constituted "security risks" for the government because they were easily subject to blackmail. But no single homosexual in the State Department was ever charged with disloyalty, and no case of disloyalty was revealed or reported.

Men discharged from the United States forces for homosexual reasons are barred from receiving any and all government benefits under the G.I. Bill of Rights, except those specially granted by Act of Congress. They can enjoy no government-subsidised education, no business or home loans, no bonus. No other medically discharged men have been so shabbily treated. Yet homosexuals in the United States forces have included men of all ranks; many were cited for unusual bravery; others were wounded, killed, and honoured with the most coveted medals. Homosexuality is more prevalent in the armed forces of any country than in civilian life. Homosexuals exist in all walks of American life, as in all other countries. The fact that the majority lead quiet, unsensational lives, means that their countrymen simply don't know that so many of their fellows are "gay".[1]

As the American writer Donald Webster Cory has pointed out, the laws against homosexuality could not be sustained if it were flagrantly apparent that millions of human beings in all walks of life were affected.

Cory [2] quotes the example of two male lovers whose "marriage" was more than ten years old when he described it. In Claude's family, John is accepted not only as the business partner but even, in a rather jocular fashion, as Claude's lover. In fact Claude's elder sister has introduced John as her brother-in-law on more than one occasion. The laughter that greets such a remark is not scornful nor pitying, but friendly and compassionate.

Both men have a wide circle of friends. Their appearance, voices and mannerisms are thoroughly masculine. Their love started at college. After graduation they were separated in the war, but afterwards they settled down as business partners. By openly proclaiming their methods of living they relieved themselves of tensions and the need for hypocrisy and pretence and shame.

It seems clear that there is as much ignorance about homosexuals in America as in Britain. The legend that "queers" are all effeminate "nancies" and "fairies" persists in the United States. "He's just like a woman" is a masculine taunt indicating that a woman is an inferior being, and that a man should have no feminine characteristics.

Life in the United States is difficult for most homosexuals, as in Britain. In most states, the laws against practising homosexuals are severe. Cory has revealed that there are "such large numbers of corrupt police who victimise homosexuals that some law-enforcement agencies actually have secret members entrusted with

[1] The American slang word for homosexuality is *gay*. Most homosexuals know it. Their word for heterosexual or "normal" is *straight*. Although *gay* is used throughout the United States and Canada, the word *straight* is hardly known on the west coast, where a more familiar word is *jam*. The American equivalent of the English term *pansy* is *fairy*; both originally indicated effeminacy, but are now used indiscriminately to denote a homosexual.

[2] *The Homosexual Outlook,* by Donald Webster Cory.

the task of discovering extortion practised by the officers of the law."

An article in the American magazine *Cosmopolitan* (May 1961) revealed, "It may come as a surprise to the sophisticates to learn that in the main the most successful male models *aren't* homosexual. The people who hire them, the advertisement agency executives and the T.V. casting girls are too aware of this trait, and they try to steer clear of it. They don't want the sturdy, male-looking adventurer with the tattoo just below his rolled-up corduroy shirt to be hauled into court for reasons which would certainly do their advertiser-clients no good in the public-relations department."

It seems clear that in the United States a large group of people is prevented from obtaining work to which it is well fitted because of the ignorance of the public and the savage and intolerant law which prevails.

While the Western world mainly rejects homosexuality, the Eastern world (with the possible exception of the Soviet Union, which is under the influence of revolutionary puritanism) is inclined to accept it. In many parts of the East, where sexual passion is regarded as no more than a pleasurable pastime, homosexual practices are regarded as an additional emotional outlet. Homosexual behaviour creates no problems, and is not regarded as abnormal, any more than it was in the golden days of Ancient Greece. I have seen young men and boys walking hand in hand in such cities as Damascus, Aleppo, Beirut, Baghdad and Teheran. No doubt when they are twenty-two or three these youngsters will be married, with children. But now, while they are sixteen or seventeen or more, they enjoy homosexual friendships which are accepted by their parents and by all adults as being quite normal and only to be expected.

There is no doubt that these youngsters are entirely masculine, and very virile. They are in fact tough fighters and have been hardened by lack of Westernised comforts. There is no trace of effeminacy in such relationships, but affection and comradeship are constantly present. In the old world, homosexuality is accepted as part of the comradeship of life.

In modern Israel, one of the youngest and yet most progressive countries in the world, the laws against homosexuality are the same as in Britain, but they are hardly ever applied. So there are no homosexual "criminals" and there is no problem to waste the time of the State and the police. If only this were true of Britain and the United States!

CHAPTER 7

Blackmail and Suicide

I

MORE homosexuals than ever before are being robbed, blackmailed, beaten up, or are receiving threatening letters. Many "queer" lives end in suicide. Let me tell you why.

Because of the existing laws against us, we fall easy prey to crooks. The late Lord Jowett, Lord Chancellor from 1945 to 1952, revealed in 1954 that when he became Attorney-General (in 1929) he was impressed with the fact that "a very large percentage of blackmail cases—nearly 90 per cent of them—were cases in which the person blackmailed had been guilty of homosexual practices with an adult person".

Blackmailers know the law is strongly against us, so they reap rich rewards by threatening their victims with exposure. And because this can mean losing a job, disgrace, and risking family life, many men pay up.[1]

Some blackmailers start early in life. At Maidstone in 1947 a boy of sixteen was fined £10 for blackmailing a man of twenty-five. It was stated that the boy had first demanded money from men when he was twelve.

[1] See the film *Victim*.

In London a coloured man was recently sent to jail for seven years for demanding money with menaces from a retired army captain. In two and a half years he had extracted £8,800 from his victim.

A friend of mine paid £80, and lost his gold watch, to a young blackmailer he foolishly met on Hampstead Heath. When the youth demanded a further £5, my friend came to me for advice. He was frightened that his mother would receive a letter revealing that he was homosexual; he knew she would never understand. I told him to go to Scotland Yard, where I knew a "queer" detective. A meeting was arranged outside Green Park tube station. The police grabbed the blackmailer as he was handed an envelope containing dummy money. No action was taken against my friend. But all "queers" are not so fortunate. It is certainly not always safe for a blackmailed homosexual to report the circumstances to the police, since in a number of recent cases (1962) the victim has been prosecuted for indecency while the criminal has gone free.

In April 1960 two men were charged with homosexual behaviour after one of them had complained that the other was trying to blackmail him. No charge of blackmail was preferred. A year earlier the Home Secretary had made it clear that homosexuals who report blackmail can be given no guarantee that they themselves will not be prosecuted. The law therefore offers protection to the blackmailer.

Sometimes blackmail is levied by unexpected people. At Sunderland, in 1958, a twenty-two-year-old policeman was sent to jail for four years for demanding £5 each from two men, one aged seventy-three, whom he had met in a public lavatory. And at Maidstone a twenty-three-year-old labourer went to jail for three years, having formed the habit of meeting men by chance in public lavatories, where he accused them of improper conduct and demanded money.

In many cases where "queers" are blackmailed or robbed, the assailant, however "normal" he may appear, first indulges in a sex act with his victim. In 1958, in Sydney, Australia, a young man was found dead in a public park. Three youths, charged with his murder, claimed their victim was homosexual, and said they had hit him because they were outraged by his behaviour. But medical examination of the body showed that at least one if not all three of the youths had intercourse with the man before killing him. Each was sentenced to fifteen years' imprisonment for manslaughter.

At Staffordshire Assizes in 1957, Mr Justice Stable said that he knew of many cases where people were driven to the verge of suicide and beyond by this disgusting, cowardly way of getting money. Suicide figures among homosexuals are in fact very high, and appear to be on the increase. I recently wrote down the names of homosexuals whom I have personally known during the last twenty years, whose lives have ended in suicide. I counted eleven people.

When nine men and two youths of seventeen were brought before the Evesham Magistrates' Court in April 1956 on charges of indecency a defending solicitor revealed that three others who might have been before the court had committed suicide. After police questioning one man had gassed himself, and another, a married man with three children, lay down on a railway line and was killed. Of the eleven men actually summoned, one old man of eighty-one was taken to hospital with cerebral haemorrhage before a verdict could be given.

If I suggest that a law which leads to such terrible tragedies is inhuman and therefore thoroughly bad, I think I do not overstate our case.

II

Most "queers" experience difficulties of adjustment, especially when they are young, which impose a great strain on their lives. Loneliness in later life is often difficult to bear. Sometimes the whole world, including our own families, seems against us. And on some occasions the threat of exposure or police prosecution drives us to sudden suicide.

At Bilston, Staffordshire, two friends who lived together were recently questioned by detectives about "certain unnatural sexual offences". One man was a widower of sixty-six, the other was forty-one. Both strongly denied the allegations which concerned no one but themselves, but they felt unable to face a criminal charge. They therefore made a suicide pact and gassed themselves. The torment in the minds of people forced to endure such persecution is difficult to imagine, but these cases are frequent, and are not always fully reported in local newspapers.

These suicide victims are often valuable members of the community. In Windsor, Australia, the brilliant cancer research scientist Dr Ferdinand Duval leapt to his death from an open window rather than face charges involving his men friends. From admissions he made to the police, many prominent people in New South Wales were involved in a homosexual "witch-hunt". Aged forty-five, Dr Duval was regarded as one of the most promising medical scientists in Australia.

Police "witch-hunts" frequently end in suicide. After being interviewed by detectives, a forty-two-year-old barman gassed himself in his bedroom. Only five days later his friend, a forty-six-year-old carpenter, who had also been interviewed, threw himself under a train, leaving a widow and three children. And in December 1959 a young man of twenty-one burned himself to death after several unsuccessful attempts to commit suicide following a police prosecution.

Day after day the homosexual suicides continue. At Chisledon a twenty-three-year-old Cornish soldier hanged himself in a disused barrack room after being released on bail following a police summons alleging indecency at Bath. A Blackpool theatre electrician killed himself on the day he should have appeared in court. A school teacher, committed on trial at Plymouth, threw himself under a train at Hendon. And a Norwood man who tried to gas himself after being charged with gross indecency was sent for trial on a further charge of attempted suicide.

One of the most shocking cases of recent years involved a seventeen-year-old Durham boy who was charged with offences involving indecency with men. Overcome by a situation which he could not explain, with no one to help him, he took his raincoat belt and hanged himself in his prison cell.

Speaking of this case, Mr Justice Elwes did not hesitate to say what he thought. "In a decent world," he said, "an adolescent would not be prosecuted for a criminal charge arising out of a sexual offence. He would be handed over to some intelligent, sympathetic person who would help him out of his difficulties. This tragedy brings into relief these matters. One can only hope that the way of reform will be made easier by this dreadful thing."

But will it? I have suggested that there are at least a million male homosexuals in Britain today. But the experience of an eminent doctor over the past thirty years has convinced him that there are as many as between one and a half million and two million men in these islands who are predominantly homosexual. No-one knows the exact figure, we can only guess. But investigations in several European and other countries show that the percentage figures vary little from country to country.

Whatever our number in Britain, we know that no reform is planned, and that the present Conservative Government [1] is against changing the old law. Meanwhile, blackmailers may safely rob us, and the suicide rate remains shockingly high.

We lag far behind Denmark, Holland, Austria, Switzerland, and other enlightened countries, where homosexuality is recognised not as a crime but as a condition of life, common in varying degrees to all humans and animals. Austria recently changed the law on Wolfenden lines. Why can't it happen here?

No matter how deep and honest and rewarding our love for our own kind, must we continue to end up in court, in the newspapers, in public disgrace, and possibly be driven to suicide?

[1] In 1962.

CHAPTER 8

The Policeman at the Door

I

IN May 1958 the Homosexual Law Reform Society was formed to fight the existing law against us. Like all movements attempting to help people—such as the campaigns against slavery and sweated labour and to prevent children from being exploited in mines and factories—the Society has met with considerable opposition. But its active supporters include the Archbishops of Canterbury and York, four bishops of the Church of England, fifteen Members of Parliament, and many thousands of other people.

The Society claims that it is intolerable that we homosexuals are condemned to live in fear of the law simply because of our emotional feelings, which are not of our choosing. It says we should be accepted, and encouraged to take our rightful place in the community with the least possible friction, just as we are accepted in the vast majority of countries. Without doubt, this must happen one day, but meanwhile the process is hindered by the barbaric treatment which the law now prescribes.

It is unexpected—and as far as I know, unique—to find an organisation such as this run by heterosexuals. Yet their view is that a change in the law is vital to many more than the existing minority of homosexuals; for one family in every ten or eleven is likely to contain a homosexual child, and under the existing law in Britain these children are *born* criminals.

The Society has headquarters in London, from where it sends out literature, organises lectures and discussions, writes letters and articles for newspapers, and endeavours in every way to influence public opinion to bring about a reform in the law and so to lessen the burden which most of us "queers" are forced to endure. Its work is carried out by unpaid volunteers, and it relies entirely on *you* for subscriptions, donations, and active support.

Men often go to the Society for advice, which is never refused if help can be given or found. But many of those who telephone or call are homosexuals who seek aid, often desperately, when it is too late. Some of these are the more ignorant or uninformed "queers" who have unfortunately been unable to find guidance, or have been content to live promiscuous lives in the shadow of a severe law which has eventually overwhelmed them. Others have just been unlucky, or have fallen into traps. There are certainly many more ignorant "queers" in Britain than you would imagine, especially young ones. In the smaller towns in the provinces there are many youths, unmistakably and unchangeably "queer", who are growing up as homosexuals but with very little idea of the truth about themselves or their condition. They have never been able to talk about their emotional and sexual problems with anyone but their own kind, and so the ignorance has spread. Seldom are such subjects discussed with parents, brothers, sisters, friends, schoolmasters, doctors, or local clergy. Most parents are so ignorant of the basic facts about homosexuality that their advice would be useless, if it were not actually damaging. And so the ignorance is handed down from generation to generation. And large numbers of young men develop a completely one-sided view of their condition, and all their sexual urges go underground and are repressed.

But not always. Because the law is so harsh against us, and because so-called "normal" people remain ignorant, many of us flaunt our "queerness", behaving in an abandoned and affected way. This happens especially among youths who have never known a restraining influence, and have been poorly educated.

"She's a bitch," one will say of another, and the expression takes on a new and slightly sinister meaning.

But although homosexuality is as widespread in the densely populated areas of the north and midlands as anywhere else, it usually stays where you are unlikely to notice it in the big towns, unless you are told about it or shown it. In a town like Bolton in Lancashire, or great cities like Leeds and Sheffield in Yorkshire, or Newcastle or Nottingham, there are countless "queers", many known to one another, living under each other's influence for better or for worse, strictly *outside* the community, picking up habits and expressions and ideas and even modes of dress from one another, but nearly all removed from other influences because society makes no attempt to invite them in. The place for us, say the authorities, is jail.

When one of these men makes a mistake and falls foul of the police, he sometimes hears, if he is lucky, of the existence of the Society. Perhaps a friend knows about it or someone has seen an advertisement in a newspaper. Then the unfortunate victim, usually feeling very sorry for himself and probably in trouble for the first time in his life, hears with some surprise that there actually exists a group of people who *care* about what he thinks and how he feels and even understands what he has himself never fully understood, why he is different from the others around him, an unconventional life apart.

Let us look at one of these experiences and see what happens. It cannot be an entirely true story because the Society deals with its visitors and correspondents in confidence, but it can be a composite picture of a number of people, and it is typical of the many instances in which men seek help from this organisation, the only one of its kind, which is pledged to assist but must not break the law in doing so.

Tony is under twenty-one, tall, slim, and fair, and he works as a clerk in the office of a large factory in Milltown. He has known for some time that he is somehow different, that he has no liking for girls, little interest in the activities of his mates, and not much in common with other fellows of his age. If he had been sensible he would already have left Milltown, for there isn't much about the place which suits his temperament. Perhaps he will, one day. He should go to sea, or join the Army, or live in a bigger town. But he has stayed where he was born, in the dingy little house near the railway arches at the end of Waterloo Street, where you can hear the express trains roaring their way north towards Scotland, and south towards London. He works in the same factory as his father, and it's a dull job.

Tony's elder brother is a steward on a liner, his elder sister is married to a bookmaker in Lancashire, and he looks like staying on for ever in the house, while his parents get older. It seems generally accepted that one day he will meet the right girl and get married, but he's not so sure. He thinks his brother suspects his inclinations, but nothing has ever been said. And so the years have drifted by, and although he is still very young, there doesn't appear to be any escape.

The house has no bathroom but it is always spotlessly clean and his mother never stops scrubbing and polishing, and whitewashing the front step, and washing clothes. There's not a lot of money about, but the boy manages to spend four or five times as much on clothes as his father; he favours pointed shoes, short topcoats, and smart hair styles, and he always looks neat and clean. His father says he looks like a pouf, dressed up like that.

Like many other youngsters at school he had "messed around", but he didn't know he was really "queer" until he was seventeen, when he met a boy who worked in the council offices, and started going around with him. When they went to Blackpool together on holiday no-one thought it strange. Then they drifted apart and he met someone else, but it isn't easy for friendships of that kind to flourish in Milltown, there is nowhere much to go except the cinema and the park or the coffee bar. Then came George, and suddenly life was quite different.

George was a good deal older, nearly thirty, and he had been well educated at a Scottish grammar school. He worked in a local office and he was a cut above nearly everyone that Tony had known. He had a large room in a pleasant house on the edge of the town, the top end they called it, and there was a television set, a record player, and reproductions of famous paintings on the walls. Tony stayed there with him in the evenings and together they listened to concerts and talked about books and the theatre, in which George was passionately interested. What he said seemed good common-sense and he was able to convince Tony that there really wasn't anything odd about their relationship. They went up to London together, to the theatre, and had supper in a restaurant in Soho, and stayed together in an hotel, and it wasn't long before the boy realised that he was in love with George, very deeply. Not only because the older man was pleasant-looking, and good company, but because he had helped him and had given him a great feeling of peace and contentment, which he had never known before.

Until he met George, Tony had always considered his secret shameful, something to be hidden away in the dark recesses of the mind. He had even thought, when he was nearly eighteen, that he wasn't quite right in the head, that he was unbalanced. Not actually mad, but certainly odd. "Queerness" was a mental complaint, wasn't it? That was how it got its name. He had believed this until the evening when they were sitting listening to a Brahms record, and he expressed his fears. He'd never talked about it before, in all his twenty-one years, but for the last four years he'd thought about it a good deal. George listened, and then went over to the bookshelf and came back with an open book showing a colour plate of a painting of Michelangelo.

"Do you think that was painted by someone who was barmy?" he asked. "I wouldn't mind being round the bend if I could paint like that."

In London they met some of George's friends, amusing and pleasant and kind, and certainly quite sane, although they were all homosexuals. But of course this new, bright world in which inhibitions vanished had to be kept apart from Waterloo Street. It was like having two completely different lives. And he couldn't discuss the truth about George with anyone.

"You're seeing a lot of that fellow," his mother had said.

"He's all right," said Tony. You always made understatements in Milltown.

She said, "I don't know why you don't find yourself a nice girl, there are plenty around. You used to like Gladys Smith."

"When I was a kid," he replied. How could he do anything but hide the truth? Lies came naturally. He was sure his parents wouldn't understand, and never in a hundred years could he tell his father. There was very little sympathy between them. His mother had once told him that just before he was born, the old man had said he hoped for a girl. In the circumstances, that was rather funny. But he had never hit it off with his father, they had almost nothing in common. What could you share with a father who talked only about the good old days before the war, when cigarettes were twenty for elevenpence-halfpenny, and then spent most of his spare time in the pub on the corner? So there had been no-one to explain to him, when he was fifteen or sixteen, why he wasn't quite like Sam and Jimmy and Bill along the street, why he felt differently, why he enjoyed habits which some of his friends also practised but which others called "dirty". Even George's reassurance, when it came, hadn't quite convinced him that homosexuality wasn't wrong, wasn't a sin.

Sometimes there were reports in the Sunday newspapers. On the front page would be a picture of the Queen, or Prince Charles, or Princess Margaret. Inside, on page two, would be the headlines which several million readers would seek :

VICAR PLEADS GUILTY
"REVOLTING" SAYS JUDGE

Father, reading the paper in front of the fire while waiting for the Sunday dinner, would turn the page over and sneer.

"I don't know why they don't do something about these

people," he says. "I'd give them a good dose of the cat if I was a judge. Filthy beasts."

How could you tell him, after that, that you understood the wretched man's failing, because you had similar inclinations? One couldn't, of course. It was unthinkable. His father would never understand, he was an uneducated working man. Perhaps that was the trouble, so many people in Britain had little or no education. They were quite content to sit night after night with their eyes glued to the telly, watching American cowboy films, but they knew almost nothing about the world around them. How could they be expected to cope with such a complex problem as homosexuality in their homes when most of them couldn't successfully control their own so-called "normal" married lives? Weren't there always rows in the street, and crises next door, and family disasters, and fellows running off with other people's wives, and babies coming when they weren't wanted, and sometimes a suicide in the parish to end a dreary old life which had wasted away in a grim backwater of poverty and despair? That was the pattern of Waterloo Street, in spite of the telly and the new electric washers and all the talk about better living conditions. Half the houses still had no bathrooms. If you didn't have one you just put up with it, and washed in the kitchen. If you were homosexual you also put up with it, but you couldn't mention it. No-one would understand.

II

All might have gone well if George hadn't been transferred to the firm's branch in Glasgow. They'd been together for nearly two years and had become so accustomed to one another they could almost tell what the other was thinking. But Glasgow is far from Milltown and although George wrote frequently and they arranged to go on holiday together in the summer, life for Tony suddenly became bleak and dull. Waterloo Street, with the cats scuttling along the wet, slimy pavements and the old men with asthma pushing their way into the pub on the corner, and the women queueing outside the fish and chip shop, Waterloo Street looked surprisingly dreary. He missed George's smile, and the warmth of the fire in his room, and the walks they had taken together, and the way their hands had touched in the dark privacy of the cinema.

It was worse when spring came to Milltown and the crocuses started sprouting under the beech trees in the park, and the days grew longer towards summer. If it wasn't for his mother, he kidded himself, he would have left home long ago. There was nothing between him and his father, they were poles apart.

"You behave more like a bloody girl than a man," the old boy had said. Home wasn't much fun when your father talked like that. All that jazz about being a *man*, what did it add up to except that you went down to the pub and talked a lot of rubbish about things you didn't really understand, and queued up for a football match, and feared just like everyone else that one day you might lose your job? Life was much the same, whatever you were.

Now there were temptations which the boy had never noticed before; men who walked past and turned back to look; fellows who stood around in the evening half-light at the park gates, hour after hour; an effeminate long-haired youngster in the factory canteen who grinned foolishly, and winked at him. But Tony wasn't interested, he waited for the postman's knock at the door and took George's letters upstairs and sat on his bed and read them through very slowly.

"There's another letter from Glasgow," his father had said, as if it were a crime to write or receive letters.

"Don't keep anything I write," George had told him. "Throw them away; burn them. It's safer." But it was pleasant at night, reading them over again. Tony kept them at the back of his handkerchief drawer, and they were an immense consolation that spring, when people began to move out of doors and Milltown appeared to be waking up from its long winter sleep. There were only two months to go to July and the promised holiday in the south, when suddenly the blow fell and everything came crashing down.

Tony came back to his late tea one Wednesday evening and there in the centre of the kitchen table lay his little bundle of letters, secured by a red rubber band. At first he couldn't think of anything to say, but just stood staring at them. If it ever crossed his mind that no-one had read them he knew he was wrong directly he looked at his father, sitting in front of the fire reading the newspaper. The boy still didn't know what to say, but he suddenly felt sick in his stomach and went upstairs to the lavatory where he knelt on the bare floor sweating, with his head hung over the porcelain bowl, fearful of the future, terribly afraid because everything had caught up with him at last.

When he ventured downstairs his father dropped the newspaper and said, "I was looking for a clean handkerchief." He said it as if no further explanation were needed.

"They're not yours," said Tony. "You didn't have any right——"

"Don't talk rubbish," said his father. "I should have guessed long ago. I thought as much, with all those letters arriving. I don't know what your mother'll say." He didn't look at Tony, but kept his eyes on the newspaper.

Tony said, "She doesn't have to know anything—it's nothing to do with you or her—they're private letters—it's my business——" He knew his voice sounded hysterical, high-pitched like a girl's.

"They're filthy," said his father. "If you want plain speaking, they're bloody filthy. Who sent them?"

"It's nothing to do with you," said Tony. "They're mine."

"That fellow you used to go around with, the one who went to Glasgow, wasn't it?" He rose and took the letters off the table, and then went and stood in front of the kitchen fire like a Victorian parent laying down the law to an erring son. The trouble was that he was a small man, and his slippers were shabby, and he needed a shave.

"You'll see whether it's got anything to do with me," he said. "You're under twenty-one, and you get disgusting, pansy letters from a man, sent here to *my* house. Then you turn round and say it's nothing to do with me. Whose house do you think it is, then? Who keeps you?"

"I keep myself. I pay Mum every week. My letters haven't got anything to do with you, they're private. You'd no right to take them out of my drawer."

"You listen to me," said his father. "I'll do what I bloody well like in my own house, and I don't want any cheek from you. A man who writes letters like that ought to be locked up, and I'll see that he is. We'll see what the police say about it."

"You wouldn't dare," said Tony.

"No?" said the old man. "Just wait and see."

The boy couldn't think of anything else to say without making matters worse. Everything seemed so inadequate, it was all so grossly unfair.

"But you're my father," he said at last. "I didn't ask to be born."

"I bloody well wish you hadn't been," said the old man. "Who the hell wants a flaming pansy for a son?"

They stood staring at one another and there seemed to be nothing in the room, no sink, no cupboard, no table, nothing but the two of them standing there while the clock on the mantelshelf tick noisily on. Then Tony went to the door and let himself out.

"You *bastard*," he said, as he shut the door behind him. And that night, for the first time since he was a child, he cried himself to sleep.

III

Next day his father went down to the police station during the dinner break and complained that a man had been writing indecent letters to his young son. The inspector read through the letters and noted the address on top of one of them. In his opinion they weren't indecent, but they were love letters written by an older man to a younger one and his experience of love letters was meagre. He hadn't written or received one for many years. Coming from one male to another, they disgusted him. And it occurred to him that these two men might be part of the homosexual vice ring which he believed existed in Milltown, but which eluded him. Only last week, two men had been arrested for indecency in the park, but it hadn't led to anything further.

After the inspector had put a telephone call through to the Glasgow police, George was met by a young constable as he left work on his way home. At the station they kept him for nearly two hours while an inspector and a sergeant and a plain clothes detective questioned him about his life, his habits, friends, his past, and what he had done in Milltown. How had he come to know Tony? What went on in the room on the edge of the town? What indecency had taken place? He told the truth, except that he didn't admit to any physical acts. It was just a strong friendship, he said. There wasn't anything illegal in that, was there?

It was the long-haired boy in the factory canteen who told Tony about the Homosexual Law Reform Society. Tony felt so overwhelmed by the situation that he was compelled to talk to someone, and he knew the boy was "queer".

"Blimey," said the youth. "You're in a bit of a mess, aren't you?" But he had told an older friend of his, a chemist in the town, and the man had written out the name and address of the Society on a piece of paper and suggested Tony should see them at once.

So when the police called at Waterloo Street to question him, causing quite a lot of interest by driving up in a patrol car, Tony was already on his way to London, having gone sick from work. And he was sick, he had never had such a shock in his young life. With George away the position seemed desperate.

In all the great borough of Milltown, rich with factories and businesses and shops, with its imposing town hall and new civic centre, its public services, hospitals, clinics, schools, churches, chapels, committees, clubs, and welfare organisations, its teeming tens of thousands of workers and its upper crust of wealthy industrialists and professional men and traders, there was as far as he knew no single person who could help him except the "queer" boy in the canteen who had given him the address.

"Whatever you do," the boy had said, "don't tell the police anything. They'll trap you into saying something against your friend."

George had managed to telephone Tony at the factory at four o'clock on the previous day. He said the Glasgow police hadn't been unsympathetic, and the inspector had been quite pleasant when he was sure that no offence had been committed in the city. George had answered all the questions frankly, had assured them he hadn't seduced or unduly influenced anyone, hadn't behaved promiscuously, hadn't offended anyone, and that there was no note book full of addresses. That was what the Milltown police hoped for.

The trouble was that the letters contained affectionate expressions which left no reasonable doubt about the physical position. How, worried George, had Tony so stupidly kept those damning letters instead of destroying them? George was due to return for further questioning, but no charge had yet been brought against him and if he was to be charged it would probably be in Milltown. And of course he was worried about keeping his job.

Tony felt like a rat in a sinking ship, but in the train to London he reflected that he was a jump ahead of the police. They hadn't interviewed him yet, and surely they couldn't prove anything if he denied all physical contact with George? He had hardly seen his father and they hadn't spoken since that first stormy evening. The old man would get a shock when he discovered his precious son had run away. His mother knew nothing yet, but it was only a matter of time. She had lent him a couple of pounds to help with the fare. The joke was, if this was the time for jokes, that they came out of the housekeeping money.

He found the offices of the Society in a large building in Shaftesbury Avenue. For about ten minutes he sat waiting in an outer office but it seemed more like an hour, and his heart was racing away as if he were facing a major operation or expecting the sack. The only time he had ever felt like this was when he was about thirteen, waiting for a beating from a master at school. But at last the door opened and he was asked to go into the other room.

To his surprise, the person sitting at the desk was a young woman.

"Good morning," she said. "Please sit down. Now, what's the trouble?"

At first he found it difficult to tell such an intimate story to a stranger, especially a woman, but every now and again she asked a question and it was soon obvious that she knew at least as much as he about homosexuals, and possibly more.

"And you had sexual intercourse with him?" she asked.

He hesitated, and then said, "Well, yes—I did."

"But you haven't had similar experiences with a lot of people in your town? They won't find, if they start investigating, that you are a promiscuous person?"

"No, I'm not. I haven't been with anyone for a long time, except George. That's what's unfair about it. It isn't as if I—well, you know."

"And what about your friend?"

He said, "He's the same, he never even looks at anyone else."

The young woman made some notes on a pad on the desk, and then said, "Just wait a minute and I'll see what I can do. But I must warn you it may not be very much. The police will probably ask to see you soon and you'd better know where you stand. I can't help you to break or evade the law and you'll have to take what's coming to you. All we can hope, if your case comes to court, is that the magistrate will be an enlightened one. He might be, or he might not. I'll be back in a minute."

When she had gone Tony lit a cigarette and looked around. It had been a relief, talking to her. There wasn't much to see in the room, a shelf with a few books, some filing cabinets, a cupboard, and some chairs. Then the woman returned and sat down behind the desk.

"It is Milltown, isn't it?" she asked.

"That's right."

"Near Bradley?"

"About four miles."

She said, "Then you may be in luck. We know a solicitor in Bradley, a good family solicitor with an excellent practice. He's one of our supporters. Before you go home you'd better go to Bradley and see him. We'll give you a letter. I think he'll try to help, but you'll have to tell him everything, and you must take his advice. If he can see your friend as well, he may be able to do more. But you mustn't be disappointed if he can't work miracles. Would you like to go and see him?"

He said, "Yes, I would—thanks very much."

"It may cost you something, but I'll ask him to try to keep the costs down. If he takes you on he'll represent you in court—that is, if it goes to court. Your father seems a very difficult man."

"Yes, he is. We've never got on, since I was a kid."

"I'll have the letter typed," she said. "Then you ought to get off to Bradley as soon as possible."

IV

Both men were charged with indecent behaviour over a period of two years.

"I'd like to make an example of them," the chief constable had said. "There's far too much of this kind of thing around, and it's spreading."

The case was heard in the magistrates' court at Milltown and after half an hour the bench found them both guilty and put them on probation for two years. They were lucky, they might have been sentenced to quite long terms of imprisonment. Six of the letters were read out in court by the prosecution.

"It is quite clear from the letters," said the chairman of the bench, "that homosexual acts have frequently taken place between you two men, although the letters themselves are not indecent. But there is no doubt that the acts were indecent, and that they took place over a long time. However, because of what your solicitor has said on your behalf, and since neither of you has been in trouble before, we are not willing on this occasion to send you to prison, which we think is not a suitable place for offenders of your kind. I may say that this is in spite of the recommendations of the police. Instead, you will both be placed on probation for two years. My advice is that you cease to see one another. And I warn you that if either of you comes before this or any other court again on a similar charge, the consequences may be very serious indeed."

In defending them, the solicitor from Bradley told the bench that both his clients had promised to seek medical aid. This helped to win the sympathy of the magistrates, for there was no doubt that a good psychiatrist with a real understanding of the problem could help both men to come to terms with themselves, although the chances of "curing" them were negligible. The trouble was that most of the doctors in Milltown lacked the least sympathy for homosexuality, and to tell the two friends to stay together as happy, and therefore useful, members of society would have seemed unthinkable.

The case was reported fully in the local newspaper, but the attitude of the neighbours in Waterloo Street was not quite what Tony had expected. There were one or two odd looks in the factory, but his employers never even mentioned the case, and most people went out of their way to be kinder than usual, especially the folks next door, who had troubles of their own. Families who hadn't noticed him for years now observed him, and passers-by said, "Hullo, Tony, how's things?" and the housewives at their front doors called out "Hullo, luv!" which meant quite a lot in Milltown.

Without realising it, the boy had suddenly become part of the community, a fellow sufferer with a problem. He was still too young to appreciate that in nearly every home there is some skeleton locked away in a cupboard, some tragedy, some event that isn't usually discussed, a difficulty to be solved, a secret to be kept. A simple case of homosexuality wasn't so rare, after all. And it wasn't as if young Tony was a Ted, or a hooligan, or a smash-and-grab type. In fact, most people thought him a rather pleasant young man.

The person who came out of it worst was Tony's father. People thought him very strange, to take his own son to court. But Tony's mother took it all in her stride and even volunteered the opinion that George had "looked rather handsome" in court. Then she went back to her stove and her polishing and cleaning and washing and forgot all about it. But she hardly spoke to her husband for a fortnight, and Tony didn't speak to him at all.

George returned to Glasgow, but he lost his job and was out of work for three months before he found another. But very soon people forgot about the newspaper report and when at last the period of probation ended, Tony realised that Milltown couldn't hold him any longer and that he ought to be moving out of Waterloo Street. So any day now he will be finding himself a job in one of the big cities. And I have an idea that the place he will choose will be Glasgow.

V

It could quite easily have been a true story. Cases like this, some worse and others more simple, come up before the courts with monotonous regularity. Many are extremely sordid and nearly all prove heart-breaking once the investigations have got under way.

The Society cannot always help those who telephone or write or call. Sometimes a "queer" will ring up and ask if he can be introduced to others of his kind—an impossible situation which must nevertheless be handled carefully because the caller may be desperately lonely and possibly be depressed. But of course such requests have to be politely rejected, and the true objects of the Society explained.

Occasionally, the "antis" write letters. These are the people who consider the aims of the Society anti-social, disgusting, and liable to encourage vice. Some of the abuse is pathetic, revealing complete ignorance of the truth. But most letters come from men seeking help, often too late. They are the ones with the police at the door, jobs lost, a threat of blackmail, a paragraph in a local paper, or an employer who is victimising an employee. It is extremely difficult to help some of these men when circumstances have already overtaken them. But understanding advice can sometimes be given, and a man may be encouraged to seek competent medical, spiritual, or legal help. In every case the Society tries to persuade the unfortunate man that all is not lost. And in such cases, sympathy and understanding can be of great benefit. At least, they might make the victim think twice before acting foolishly; at most they will give him strength to face the uneven battle.

Day after day they come to the offices; men who have made no serious attempt to control their lives or to channel their feelings rationally; men who have been weak, and seek help only when actually in trouble; men who have suddenly given way to temptation. A hand moving over a leg in a cinema, a protest to the manager, a telephone call to the police, and within a few minutes a career and sometimes a life is in jeopardy. People shouldn't behave like that, but they do. They aren't taught about such things in school or at home, and what they do know about the facts of life has usually been picked up in the school playground or on the canal banks or at street corners. The shock, the tears at night, the humiliation and gossip, the friends lost, all because a hand was foolishly moved a few inches in a cinema. Then the Society is expected to provide the solution to a problem which the nation ignores. And, surprisingly, it often does.

Under the present law very little *can* be done to help homosexuals to adjust themselves without the risk of going against the law in some way. The Society must never conceal facts from the police, must never encourage illegal acts, or condone crime. All it can do in most of these distressing cases is to act as counsellor and guide, relying on the experience of experts in an effort to set the unfortunate or foolish victim of circumstances, which are often beyond his control, along a path which has at the end some visible ray of light, some hope, some prospect from which the pattern of the future does not look too appalling.

It should not be necessary for a small organisation, supported entirely by voluntary subscriptions, to be faced with such terrible problems. But almost no-one else takes them on, and apart from the work being done by the Society and its supporters, I see very little hope for homosexuals in Britain. And that means homosexuals yet unborn, which works out at one child in every ten or eleven families. If there is ever a change in the law, backed by public opinion, it is the Homosexual Law Reform Society who will deserve our thanks. Meanwhile, it needs your active support, no matter who you are.

CHAPTER 9

Change the Law!

I

IT is of course the duty of the police to preserve public order and decency. It therefore follows that when homosexual behaviour takes place *in public* or in a place where it might affect public opinion, it should be dealt with by the criminal law. But should the law interfere with what two consenting adults do in the privacy of a bedroom?

One of the principal recommendations of the Wolfenden Report remains only a forlorn hope:

> "We do not think that it is proper for the law to concern itself with what a man does in private unless it can be shown to be so contrary to the public good that the law ought to intervene in its function as the guardian of that public good."

What has been done about this recommendation? Nothing!

In England and Wales during the three years ended March 1956 no fewer than 480 men aged twenty-one and over were convicted of offences committed *in private* with consenting partners also aged twenty-one or over. The convictions continue, although it took Sir John Wolfenden and a Home Office committee three years to decide, by a majority of twelve to one votes, that homosexual behaviour between consenting adults over twenty-one in private should NOT be criminal and subject to prosecution. But Sir John and the experts were wasting their time. The Government intends to do nothing about the recommendation, although it involves the lives of at least a million men—and some say nearer two million.

So a primitive law remains, which can easily send *your* son or nephew or brother to prison for the so-called "crime" of having been born a little different from most people. And different in only *one* respect.

You may say, "But *he* isn't like that."

Isn't he? Judging by the numbers of us in Britain, and in every other country, we must be related to some people, somewhere, if not to you personally.

Is opinion really so strongly against us? There has never been a public vote on the subject. Do persons like Mr John Gordon in the London *Sunday Express* really represent the true feelings of the masses of the people, when they attack us and call us "filthy perverts"? In July 1960 the *Sunday Express*, noting Parliament's decision to ignore the Wolfenden recommendation, said, "there never was any real demand for a fresh enquiry into this sordid subject . . . by decisively rejecting the pleas of perverts, Parliament has disposed of this matter once and for all."

Once and for all! And something like a million souls are involved and affected!

No doubt Mr Gordon's solution is simple. Perhaps he would like over a million people sent to prison, possibly for life. This may have been Hitler's method of dealing with minorities—it was not only the Jews but also the homosexuals and Jehovah's Witnesses and Quakers who found themselves in Dachau. But it simply can't be done in a civilised country.

What a pity that we homosexuals continue to buy and read that seemingly biased, uninformed, and ignorant paper, which dismisses something like one twenty-fifth of the male population of Britain as "perverts", and sets back the clock to medieval ignorance and superstition. What makes homosexuality seem sordid except a law—not introduced until 1885—which calls it a criminal vice? Giving a dog a bad name does not stop it barking.

The *Sunday Express* is quite wrong in saying that there "never was any real demand for a fresh enquiry". Support for a change in the law has come from many quarters. The Church of England has voted for it, through the Church Assembly. Both archbishops have approved the idea of a change. The Methodist Conference, a specially appointed Roman Catholic Committee, and the Bow Group in the Conservative Party have all recommended changing the law. And in 1947, the National League of Young Liberals called the existing law "a barbarous remnant of an antediluvian moral code based on retribution rather than reform".

Whatever the *Sunday Express* thinks, there is strong evidence of a very large demand for reform. And if some of the sad, unhappy facts which I have revealed are more widely known, I hope the demand may increase.

The alternative to reform is a continuation of the anti-social conditions under which we homosexuals are forced to live, half in secret, frustrated, and fearful of exposure. More blackmail, more prison sentences, more family disgrace, more suicides, more importuning on the streets, and further misery for relations and friends.

Britain, it is sometimes claimed, is the champion of freedom. But her homosexuals are chained, and constantly insulted. I am tempted to ask Mr Gordon if any homosexuals are employed by the group of newspapers for which he works? I can think of only three whom I know personally, but on the law of averages there must be several more, helping to run this vigorous newspaper group. What would Mr Gordon do—kick them out? Strange that Mr Gordon should have this blind spot, because on most subjects he is a capable and readable journalist. But on the question of homosexuality he simply does not know what he is writing about.

Must we continue to endure not only the bigotry of ignorant small-town gossipers but also the vicious comments of ill-informed newspapers and sensational journalists? Why shouldn't we be recognised and accepted as a minority group so that we may be helped to lead full, happy lives?

Intelligent opinion is very firmly in favour of legal reform, and a change in the law has been approved by most of the informed newspapers and journals in Britain, including *The Times, The Guardian, The Daily Telegraph, The Observer, The Sunday Times, Reynolds News, The Spectator, The New Statesman, The Church of England Newspaper, The Economist, The Lancet,* and *The Daily Mirror.* They reflect all shades of public opinion, and may be said to represent the nation.

In March 1958, thirty-three distinguished people wrote to *The Times* urging reform. Later, a group of eminent married women wrote another letter demanding a change in the law.

Kingsley Martin, the former editor of *The New Statesman,* has said:

> I can find actually no real argument in favour of the present law except that when Sunday newspapers don't know how to amuse us because we have behaved ourselves unusually well, there's been no particular amount of murder, rape or sudden death during the week, then there is always the trial of Oscar Wilde in a pigeon hole which can be brought out to amuse us on Sunday. But apart from some reason of that kind I can find no argument in favour of the present law.

I have attempted to show in this short book that some homosexuals behave badly, and are promiscuous. But we are certainly not more promiscuous than *you* would be if you were forced to live under similar conditions of loneliness and sexual insecurity.

Fornication, adultery, rape, even murder, are discussed calmly and objectively every day. It is time that homosexuality was also freely discussed, so that we may be encouraged to play an open, constructive part in the life of the community, to which we already contribute a great deal. We should not be made to feel guilty of something beyond our control.

If the Wolfenden recommendations were adopted there would be no extra danger of young people being corrupted, because the report advocates—and the law could enforce—severe penalties against men committing sexual offences against young people. Homosexuals know that very few of us are interested in very young people, just as few so-called "normal" men are sexually attracted by little girls. In fact, there are few cases in which young boys are assaulted by men, but instances of little girls being attacked by so-called "normal" men appear to have increased lately.

In Britain, the upper classes have always regarded their own homosexuals with tolerance. It is easier for a homosexual than for a co-respondent in a divorce case to enter the Royal Enclosure at Ascot. But there is too often one law for the rich and another for the poor or uninfluential or inexperienced homosexual.

A homosexual doctor (writing in *The Lancet* in 1959) has said, "It is my considered opinion that the cause of homosexuality is still unknown. One day the heterosexual man finds he has heterosexual desires; one day the homosexual man, usually to his embarrassment and distress, finds he has homosexual desires. Neither has had the slightest choice in his sexual orientation."

A man who is completely homosexual cannot have satisfactory sexual relations with a woman. And no doctor can alter this. In fact, the best course is usually for the patient to be persuaded that his homosexuality is not wrong, but that he must adjust himself to his condition and live a decent, moral, full life without hurting anyone. How many doctors would give this advice to a "queer" patient?

Many of us are so frightened of public opinion (especially those of us who have not met many others like us) that we get married. The result is often disastrous, and such marriages, which are more frequent than one might suspect, are usually doomed to failure. Sexual happiness eludes such relationships. And the wife is faced, sooner or later, with the terrible choice of continuing a not completely satisfactory union, or of exposing her husband to the risk of criminal proceedings. One such wife was so horrified at discovering her husband's homosexual condition that she stabbed her baby to death "so he should not become a pervert". Poor woman, homosexuality is not hereditary. The chances of her son being "queer" were the same as for any other child—about one in every twenty-five.

Homosexuality is usually determined early in life. Some people unexpectedly develop tendencies in middle-age or late in life, but this is rare. The experts still don't know enough about us to be certain what causes our condition. But if your son or daughter shows signs of homosexuality there is very little you can do about it, except help. The child is yours. If you pretend not to know, he may feel guilty, and will be forced to keep up pretences and to lie. But if you share the problem honestly, at least he won't feel unwanted. And this, after all, is the test of family affection. He didn't ask you to bring him into the world.

Homosexuals really need help and advice when they are young, and are forming the pattern of their lives. For them, the teenage-time may appear full of pitfalls. For a while they believe they are the only people in the world to feel as they do. Often there is no-one with whom they can discuss their problems which, being sexual and social, appear enormously important. Emotionally, young people find it difficult to deal with homosexual problems when they are alone.

In countries where homosexuality is accepted as a condition of life there is no "queer" problem. I have pointed out that in the East it has been accepted since the creation of man, and is not considered unusual. When the British and American troops invaded North Africa in 1942 the U.S. Army issued a booklet about the Arabs. This said that if two Arabs were seen holding hands, it did not mean they were "queer"! Homosexuals will recognise the ignorance and bias behind such a misleading statement, because throughout the East and Middle East, male friends have always held hands, in token of an affection which most certainly has, in varying degrees, *some* homosexual basis.

What is the so-called "normal" society from which we homosexuals are barred? Is it any more righteous or moral than the life we secretly live? Many homosexuals consider it a world full of unfaithfulness, unhappy marriages, and prostitution. Isn't one out of every ten children born in Britain illegitimate? Looking around, do so-called "normal" people really lead such exemplary lives that the other one twenty-fifth of the population must be condemned because it doesn't share the same feelings?

The kind of vicious persecution which we think monstrous is the recent case of a young man sent to prison for a homosexual offence committed *three years previously* in private. In the meantime he had ceased all "queer" practices, had married, and was the father of a child. He was therefore not even fundamentally, totally, homosexual. But he was sent to gaol, presumably because his behaviour was still considered "immoral", three years later.

Many people claim that we "offend against morality". But everyone has different ideas of what is moral and what is not. Three British youths in Barcelona were arrested at mid-day by the Spanish police for "conduct against public morality". But what were they doing that was so immoral? Nothing but wearing bathing shorts in the street, with shirts flung over their shoulders. They spent the night in prison. But in Spain it is *not* a crime for two consenting adult males to have sexual intercourse in private.

Kingsley Martin has explained, "Those of us who are repelled by homosexuality personally, because we don't happen to feel that way, I think rather lack imagination sometimes about what it must be like to be a real homosexual. There are of course some people who are not real homosexuals; who pretend to be for various reasons. But for people who are real homosexuals, who are said to be two or three per cent of the population, or who have become so in adolescence—for those people I've sometimes thought what an extraordinary amount of discipline is demanded of them. Supposing I, all my life—I'll just think of myself, and you think of yourself at the same time and in the same way—supposing that I'd always had to bathe, to use the same lavatories, same bathrooms, to do all the intimate things of life with people of the other sex. Well, I for my part have no doubt at all I should have been in prison a very long time ago."

It is not only judges and magistrates who are at fault. The Wolfenden Report suggested that the Press might do much towards the education of public opinion by ensuring that reports of court cases concerning homosexual offences should be treated in the same way as matrimonial cases are treated; for there is little doubt that the influence of detailed reports of such cases is considerable, and almost wholly bad. It is impossible in the kind of short news report which the *News of the World* publishes (but which now less frequently appears in that newspaper) for the *whole* true story to be printed. A brief act of so-called "indecency", a comment by the judge or magistrate, and a prison sentence or fine—behind the ten or twenty lines in the column there is nearly always a sad, human story. The publication of such reports leads only to further tragedy and degradation.

We homosexuals do not expect complete licence, but we believe we should enjoy the same freedom to make moral choices about our private lives as is granted to most people without question, as a natural right.

A man may steal another man's wife, commit adultery, bring an illegitimate child into the world, and so upset three lives. Yet he couldn't even be fined five shillings. But for having lived for twenty-two years with one man—I believe to the advantage of both our characters—I could go to prison *tomorrow.*

Under our present law, a man who engages in homosexual activities, even in private, is as much a criminal as a burglar or a pickpocket or a blackmailer. Finding himself outside the law, condemned by this out-dated expression of the social will, he is sometimes inclined to question the foundations of the law, and may become anti-social, and a nuisance to the community. Thus, the homosexual expression for the police is "Lilly-Law", showing a contempt for the forces of law and order which persecute us.

The real problem of the homosexual is not psychological, but religious if he is a Christian, and social if he is British, or American, or a West German. Many Churches consider him a sinner; the State brands him as a perverted criminal. The homosexual born a Dane or a Dutchman or a Norwegian or an Austrian is much more fortunate, for he finds himself in an understanding community.

If more people face the facts about homosexuality, and study it, we shall be half-way to changing a law which viciously persecutes a minority, wastes the time of the courts and the police, and causes nothing but unhappiness—in the name of retribution. For there is no cure known to man.

Who are the people who so viciously attack us?

J. B. Priestley has said that he notices the loudest and bitterest denunciations of homosexuality coming not from men who enjoy the company of women but from men who are always running away from women, hurrying into their clubs, organising stag parties and staying up late with "the boys".

"There is," he says, "something unpleasant, hysterical, about their jeers and shouts and cries of vengeance, coming from some division in their own natures. It is they who are always making clear to us, and then condemning, the way in which homosexuals boost each other, especially in the arts. They forget that hunted men cannot help having a fellow-feeling. It is they and their lawyers and their police who have created, if it exists, any homosexual secret society of mutual aid. Change the law, purify that murky atmosphere, bring Britain into line with civilisation and this bogey, with many others, will vanish."

Now Mr Priestley is not only a fine novelist, but a man of the world and a writer with a strong social conscience. His family background and the undeniable and obvious normality of his own life makes such a contribution to our welfare extremely valuable. Consider, by comparison, the way in which John Gordon attacks us.

II

What do most homosexuals want? The answer is simple. Those of us who have considered our problems carefully want public recognition of our condition, and a change in the law so that we are not treated as criminals. We want to be allowed to live and let live and to be punished only when we really transgress against public decency. Otherwise, we wish to go unhindered about our ordinary, everyday lives without fear of persecution in the pursuit of private happiness, which is surely the right of all free men and women.

People have always been cruel about things they fear or do

not understand. It was not long ago that so-called "witches" were burned at the stake or tortured, victims of leprosy were called "unclean", lunatics were cruelly beaten so that their madness should be subdued, and even horses were publicly hanged for having caused the death of their riders. But this is the nuclear age, not the age of medieval superstition and ignorance. Fear and ignorance should not rule the lives of so many people.

Dr W. Lindsay Neustatter, at a public meeting in Caxton Hall, Westminster, in May 1960, said, "To my mind a law which produces such results is a cruel one; in addition, when it is considered that the promiscuous heterosexual is sometimes the object of admiration, and that spreading venereal disease, possibly to an unborn child, is not a legal crime, and that the Lesbian is not prosecuted, that there is every justification for saying that the present law is not only cruel, but illogical and unjust. Why, then, do so many favour it? I would submit that this is on account of prejudice, which in turn is a result of lack of knowledge about homosexuality and homosexuals. Ordinary members of the public only know what they call the 'Nancy boy'—the very obvious homosexual. I am perfectly certain that many homosexuals are never recognised as such, and it is as absurd to judge all homosexuals by the unstable 'Nancy boy', as to judge all women by prostitutes."

One thing we resent is that as people we are bracketed in a special category simply because of our sexual inclinations, as if sexual behaviour of one particular kind or another puts a man or woman into a special category, apart from nearly everyone else. It is perhaps unfortunate that the word "sexual" should be contained in the description of our condition. There are other names which are more suitable, such as the German *Urning*. For it must be realised that a great many people with homosexual inclinations never indulge in sexual intercourse with their fellows. The term "homosexual" implies a physical relationship, but in fact many such relations are never physical, being entirely mental, spiritual, or simply cases of fellowship and good comradeship. Sometimes these friendships lead to sexual expression, but very often not.

It has been said that *all* schoolmasters are homosexual. This cannot be true, but it is probably correct to say that many schoolmasters teaching boys have at least some latent homosexual instinct, or they could not continue to work with and among boys. This is of course very seldom expressed physically, and is often strictly controlled, but it is more frequently revealed emotionally and mentally.

Why are so many people repelled by homosexuality? Friendliness of boy for boy about the age of puberty is a common occurrence. Youths tend to congregate together. David and Jonathan were adolescent boys and the record of their love is held by most people to be beautiful. In most countries the Navy, Army, and Air Force provide the background in which many such friendships flourish. Boy Scouts and Boys' Brigades and youth clubs cater for this form of relationship.

There is every indication that the English public school of Victorian times, and later, was a hot-bed of homosexuality. Many popular novels about public school life are at least partly homosexual, some being almost embarrassing in their sentimentality.[1]

G. F. Lamb, in his study of English boarding school life throughout the centuries,[2] somewhat innocently suggests "there was probably little scope for homosexual practices when boys lived a communal life in which the accepted thing to do with smaller boys was to fag and bully them". Yet at many public schools there were and are no locks on the lavatory doors, to prevent homosexual liaisons. At Malvern there were no doors at all. At Charterhouse the dormitory cubicles had partitions electrically wired so that an alarm was raised if a boy entered another cubicle. But in earlier days, in many great schools, the younger boys were required to sleep two in a bed.

III

Mr James Adair, O.B.E., one of the Wolfenden committee, did not agree with the recommendations of his colleagues, that

[1] Read *The Hill*, by H. A. Vachell, or *Jeremy at Crale*, by Hugh Walpole, or some of the school novels of E. F. Benson.

[2] *The Happiest Days*, by G. F. Lamb.

homosexual acts by adults in private should not be regarded as criminal.

Said Mr Adair, "Existing homosexual trends and tendencies are currently the cause of much public concern and disgust . . ."[1] To whom? To ignorant people who know almost nothing about our condition?

Later, in his statement, Mr Adair says, "One thing seems to stand out—homosexuals, like most practices, propagate themselves." As a member of the committee who presumably had an equal chance to examine the mass of evidence, Mr Adair is singularly ill-informed. Homosexuality is not a spreading, infectious disease, like measles or chicken-pox; it is a condition. One either has homosexual inclinations or one has not. Any educated, experienced homosexual could tell Mr Adair that homosexuality isn't a cult, and doesn't spread, like a religion. That is to say, it isn't like accepting Moral Rearmament or joining a political party or becoming a Freemason; a man doesn't say, "This movement attracts me, I think I'll join." Smith doesn't become a practising homosexual because Jones is one, and has told him about it. If Smith isn't to some degree homosexual he won't take part in homosexual acts. Mr Adair makes the very common, ignorant mistake of supposing that Smith can be either persuaded or forced or seduced *against his will and better judgment* into becoming a homosexual, but any knowledgeable "queer" could tell him that this is no more likely than that a homosexual may be persuaded or forced or seduced into having intercourse with a woman. To the true homosexual, sexual relations with the opposite sex are unthinkable; just as a complete heterosexual will have no homosexual urge.

In his novel *Love Among the Ruins*, Evelyn Waugh[2] looked into the future and satirically saw a time in which homosexuals could be easily recognised because they all wore green. I wish that it could happen here, now. The public would be astonished to discover, one bright Monday morning, that an unexpectedly

[1] Wolfenden Report, 1957.
[2] *Love Among the Ruins*, by Evelyn Waugh (Chapman & Hall).

large number of people was wearing green—the bank manager, the butcher, the 'bus conductor, several passengers on the morning train, business acquaintances, perhaps an employer, the barber who has cheerfully cut your hair for ten years, and the man who sells you your evening newspapers. After all, we are everywhere.

It is a pity that we have been quite wrongly made to feel ashamed of our condition, to which no shame or feeling of guilt needs to be attached. Mr Waugh's excellent novel will no doubt remain fiction. But it would be helpful if we could collectively take some step along the path to being recognised and accepted. Even the government couldn't lock us all up at once. You would simply have to accept us. And when you had learned who we are and what we are, you would find us surprisingly respectable.

It is certainly not difficult to encounter among males a depth of affection whose duration is long-lived and faithful, devotion and sacrifice comparable to that of legal marriages, fidelity which distinguishes love and marriage from sensual pleasure, and fruitful lives based on rewarding friendships.

Bring homosexuality out into the open fresh air and encourage the medical profession to discover more about us. We are not guilty of any crime, and we are not living in 1885, when this ridiculous law against us was slipped through Parliament.

APPENDIX "A"

Some Questions and Answers

1 *Should Homosexuals have their own literature?*

Why not? If our minority is not allowed to legally express itself in its own magazines, newspapers, and other forms, and so express the homosexual viewpoint, then how about the other minorities? What about the Quakers? Why should the Jews or coloured people publish their own journals? In fact, how free *are* the people of Britain?

2 *Do Homosexuals tend to congregate together?*

Yes, in Britain, because we are social outcasts. But there is nothing socially wrong, or unusual, or dangerous, about such congregations. A homosexual who was asked by the police why he frequented clubs where men but no women assembled, replied: "Is it any stranger than being a member of *White's*, or any other London club for men only—or indeed, of being a member of the Police Force?"

3 *Are Homosexuals "artistic"?*

By no means all homosexuals have leanings towards the arts. The milkman or sailor or labourer with homosexual tendencies but only a modest education is unlikely to gain great pleasure from looking at a painting by Degas or a sculpture by Rodin. In fact, he may be rather shocked. But one reason why many of the more sensitive type of homosexuals turn to the theatre or to literature or to the Church or artistic trades and professions when they are young and seeking adjustment is because in these circles there is more tolerance than in a conventional career, or borough employment or factory life. Of course, the majority of homosexuals remain in factories or offices all their working days. It is therefore not correct to suppose that most "queers" have natural leanings towards the arts.

4 *Is homosexuality an undesirable way of life?*

Some of us would choose not to be homosexual if we had any choice in the matter because, in the world in which you force us to live, our lives often lead to unhappiness, to loneliness, and to mental frustration. Therefore, it seems clear that we deserve compassion and assistance rather than contempt and legal persecution.

5 *Who are the persecutors?*

It is characteristic of persons who are not manifestly homosexual, but whose defences against the condition are weak, to disapprove strongly of homosexual practices in others.

6 *Can a doctor help?*

Most doctors have no real knowledge of homosexuality, and many are very ignorant about the subject. As one "queer" surgeon has said, "So long as the only doctors who write on this subject are heterosexual, so long as public opinion is based on emotional prejudice, so long as the law makes it dangerous for the homosexual to express an opinion, the present profound ignorance of the subject—both inside and outside the medical profession—will continue."

There are, of course, exceptions. Some doctors have made a study of the subject. Many homosexuals bother to discover a "queer" doctor, who will with his personal experience and knowledge be more likely to help. In any case, a homosexual patient will be less likely to feel embarrassed or guilty when discussing his problems with a doctor whose condition is similar.

7 *Can it be cured?*

The word "cure" suggests disease. But homosexuality is not a disease. It is a condition, the consequence of biological or psychological factors or a combination of both. In many cases the subject no more wishes to be changed than would a heterosexual person if his cure involved becoming "queer".[1] Neither hypnosis nor psycho-analysis has been successful in dealing with this problem. It is usually better for a homosexual to adjust his mind so that he accepts his condition, instead of attempting the impossible, to become something which is unnatural to him. In his famous work *The Story of San Michele*, Dr Axel Munthe tells of meeting a young invert who had been treated by both Kraft-Ebing and Charcot and who, in the words of Munthe, was "most anxious to be cured". The doctor attempted to guide the person, through hypnosis, to the so-called accepted sexual path of life. Later, when he heard that the man had committed suicide, he said, "Had this unhappy man consulted me when I had acquired more knowledge of sexual inversion I would never have attempted the hopeless task of curing him."

8 *Is it hereditary?*

Heredity plays no part at all in homosexuality, nor does genetic abnormality or endocrine disturbance. Most homosexuals are well-adjusted and, apart from their sexual anomaly, are no different from their fellows.

9 *But are homosexuals good citizens?*

I have claimed that the majority of us are responsible, hard-working people going about our daily work just like you. I have also attempted to show that many "queers" have been, and are,

[1] From *Sex Questions and Answers*, by Fred Brown and Rudolph T. Kempton.

valuable members of the community. But Peter Wildeblood had something else to say on the subject in his excellent account of his own experiences:[1]

> I am obliged to admit that most homosexuals are furtive and irresponsible, and that if a more tolerant and just attitude towards their condition is ever adopted by this country it will not be through their efforts. On the other hand, they are perhaps not entirely to blame. Their secretiveness and cynicism are imposed upon them by the law as it now stands.

One must accept the fact that few reforms are carried out, or caused, by the people who suffer from the injustice. It was not the slaves who freed themselves, but the efforts of the reformers. Most important reforms are influenced from outside. It is therefore not surprising to note that the founders and leaders of the Homosexual Law Reform Society—the only organisation in Britain actively fighting for a change in this unjust law—are not homosexuals, but are married men and women with a social conscience and a sense of humanity.

The truth is that homosexuals would be better, more responsible citizens if they were not persecuted.

10 *What does the public say?*

I have suggested that we are accepted by the so-called "upper classes" and that the so-called "working classes", having lived close to the problem in difficult, crowded circumstances for many centuries, are not appalled by us. Consider what Wildeblood has to say about his return after being in prison for a homosexual offence, having openly admitted in court that he was a homosexual:

> I went back to Islington, feeling vaguely apprehensive about the neighbours. I had never spoken to any of them before, and I wondered how they felt about a man with an Oxford accent who came to live among them, re-decorated his house in a manner which probably struck them as obnoxious, and then proceeded to go to gaol. If they had resented my presence there, I thought, they had every opportunity of showing it now. I began to sweep and

[1] *Against the Law*, by Peter Wildeblood.

dust the rooms and clean the windows, feeling rather depressed. After a few minutes the woman next door leaned out of a window and said it was wonderful to see me back again, and was there anything she could do to help? I thanked her for her kindness and, feeling much better, went to the front door to shake the mat. Another neighbour stopped in the street, smiled, and said, "Welcome home." For the rest of the week my work was punctuated by these greetings and offers of assistance—did I want a hand with the cleaning? Was there any shopping they could do for me? They were just going to the launderette; could they take anything for me? . . . they said, "We read all about it in the papers, and we thought it was a rotten shame."

The true feelings of the masses of people in Britain have been indicated by their acceptance of the two films about Oscar Wilde, and the fictional film *Victim*. These motion pictures were widely shown and were found to be entirely acceptable both in entertainment value and the way in which they presented the homosexual condition. Yet certain sections of the public remain extremely hostile to us.

11. *What is the origin of this hostility?*

Hostility towards minority groups is taught from the time one is a child, but it is not a natural way of thinking. The Nazis were not naturally Anti-Jewish, they had to be taught and indoctrinated; there is no colour bar unless it is taught and encouraged by prejudice and laws of discrimination. And there is certainly no instinctive disgust for homosexuality, which is, and has been, accepted by many cultures. The active dislike of a majority for a minority group is simply a matter of habit and custom and teaching. If people are taught to hate they grow to hate; Jews, negroes, homosexuals are turned into scapegoats. The Germans, under Hitler, threw all their minority groups into concentration camps as being "dangerous" to the future of the German race. Thus, Jews, Quakers, Jehovah's Witnesses, homosexuals, and many others went to Dachau and other camps, and there they died. There are no concentration camps in Britain, but there are jails for homosexuals.

12. *What does the Church say?*

If by the Church you mean the Church of England, consider this extract from their report:

> It should be recognised that homosexual love is not always a genital love. The homosexual is capable of a virtuous love, as decent and as beautiful as one who is normally sexed.

13. *What is the solution?*

In nearly all cases there is no answer to the problem save tolerance on the part of the anti-homosexual groups in the community. If you are homosexual, you should try to adjust yourself sensibly to your way of life and not feel guilty that nature has fashioned you in this pattern. Perhaps you have compensations in another direction. Maybe you have an attractive personality which you might not have if you were heterosexual; or you are an artist; or likely to make a brilliant lawyer, or a faithful employee. Remember that no two trees are alike, no flowers are exactly similar. Make the most of what may sometimes seem a difficult way of life; avoid offensive or promiscuous behaviour; never subdue your true feelings simply out of fear of being misunderstood or persecuted. Live fully the life that has been chosen for you, remembering that you did not select your condition. Live decently, and do not forget that true love is usually ennobling and enriching for both partners, and can be a source of inspiration to others.

APPENDIX "B"

Homosexuality—A Short Book List

Government Papers (H.M. Stationery Office).

Cmnd. 247 : Report of the Departmental Committee on Homosexual Offences and Prostitution (Wolfenden Committee).

Hansard (Parliamentary Debates): Commons 28.4.54; Lords 19.5.54; Lords 4.12.57; Commons 26.11.58.

General

Church of England Moral Welfare Council: The Problem of Homosexuality (Church Information Board, 1954).

Church of England Moral Welfare Council: Sexual Offenders and Social Punishment (Evidence submitted to the Wolfenden Committee) (Church Information Board, 1954).

British Medical Association and Magistrates' Association: The Criminal Law and Sexual Offenders (Supplement to British Medical Journal, 12.3.49, pp. 135–140).

G. Westwood: Society and the Homosexual (Gollancz, 1952). Bibliography. Also "A Minority"—Longmans, 1960.

D. J. West: Homosexuality (Duckworth, 1955). Bibliography. Also Penguin edition, 1960.

D. W. Cory: The Homosexual Outlook (Peter Nevill, 1953). Bibliography.

E. Chesster: Live and Let Live (Heinemann, 1958).
ed. Rees and Usill: They Stand Apart—A Critical Survey of Homosexuality (Heinemann, 1955).
Rev. D. Sherwin Bailey: Homosexuality and the Western Christian Tradition (Longmans, Green, 1955).
Kenneth Walker: The Physiology of Sex (Pelican Books, 1955).
K. Walker and P. Fletcher: Sex and Society (Pelican Books, 1955).
Clifford Allen: Homosexuality, Its Nature, Causation and Treatment (Staples, 1958). Bibliography.
Peter Wildeblood: Against the Law (Weidenfeld & Nicholson, 1955, and Penguin Books).
Peter Wildeblood: A Way of Life (Weidenfeld & Nicholson, 1956).
G. Rattray Taylor: Sex in History (Thames & Hudson, 1953). Bibliography.